CLOSE TO, HIS Majesty

DAVID C. NEEDHAM
WITH
LARRY LIBBY

CLOSE
TO HIS
Majesty

AN INVITATION TO
WALK WITH GOD

MULTNOMAH · PRESS

Portland, Oregon 97266

Cover design by Bruce DeRoos

CLOSE TO HIS MAJESTY
© 1987 by Multnomah Press
Portland, Oregon 97266

Multnomah Press is a ministry of Multnomah School of the Bible, 8435 NE Glisan Street, Portland, OR 97220

Printed in the United States of America

Library of Congress Cataloging-in-Publication Data

Needham, David C., 1929-
  Close to His majesty.

  1. Trust in God—Christianity.   I. Title.
BV4637.N44   1987   231   87-11298
ISBN: 0-88070-128-5

87   88   89   90   91   92   –   10   9   8   7   6   5   4   3   2   1

CONTENTS

Chapter 1

At the Edge of Mystery

There were times when Paul had to put down his pen.

There were times when he was so overcome by what the Spirit of God was leading him to write that—for a minute or two—he couldn't add one more word.

It happens in his letter to the believers in Rome.

For three chapters he's been delving into the mysteries of God's purposes for the Jewish people. He's been talking about the strange, shocking miracle taking place in the world . . . the miracle that God would swing the door of His grace wide open to the Gentiles—non-Jews who were "without hope and without God in the world." To think God would invite the *whole world* to embrace His Son, to enter into the very heart of His affections, and to become His eternal sons and daughters!

The expert teacher Paul could have paused then to say, "There! Now you have it—the complex logic of God's purposes for the human race. Learn it well. Outline it, memorize it, and then teach it to others so they too will understand."

But no. Instead, Paul suddenly seems to shout, "Wait a minute! Time out! I can't let these words sail right by. This is too great. Too deep. Too much."

The praise and wonder well up in the battered apostle's heart and burst across the page like water through a broken levee:

> Oh, the depth of the riches of the wisdom and
>   knowledge of God!
>   How unsearchable his judgments,
>   and his paths beyond tracing out!
> "Who has known the mind of the Lord?
>   Or who has been his counselor?"
> "Who has ever given to God,
>   that God should repay him?"
> For from him and through him and to him are all things.
>   To him be the glory forever!
>
> (11:33-36 NIV)

Dropping his pen and throwing up his hands, Paul says in effect, "Oh! What a God! Who can second-guess Him? Who can begin to grasp the vastness of His truth? Who can predict what He will do? Who can trace out His logic? Who can say "Now I've got Him all figured out"?

This God we worship is a most mysterious God. Incomprehensible. He refuses to be impressed with our neat theological boxes, as though we could write down a list of statements about God, draw a circle around them, and say we have it all . . . as though His being and His ways could be bound by the limits of our intelligence.

"My thoughts are not your thoughts," God told Isaiah, "neither are your ways my ways. . . . As the heavens are higher than the earth, so are my ways higher than your ways and my thoughts than your thoughts" (55:8-9 NIV).

Not only is God higher than all our wisdom, Paul writes to the Corinthians, but even "the *foolishness* of God is wiser than man's wisdom" (1 Corinthians 1:25 NIV). In other words, if God were capable of a stupid thought—if He were—that thought would be wiser than the wisest thought man has ever conceived.

So many of us struggle with pride at this very point. Somehow we feel we deserve to know and comprehend to the same degree God knows and comprehends. As though He owes us an explanation for His actions! Yet for all eternity, you and I will bow before a God who will always be greater than our greatest thought. His love,

His patience, His holiness, His power, His purposes, and His wisdom will forever leave us in a state of astonished wonder.

Does this mean that what we say or teach about God is *wrong*? Not necessarily. Yet it does mean that our grasp of what we say or teach scarcely begins to encircle the greatness of His being. We stand only at the merest edge of comprehension.

A Hill, a Mountain . . . An Ocean

In light of this, you and I are off on a "forever adventure"—the best and highest journey any creation of God will ever know: the adventure of discovering God! This book is about that adventure.

Imagine with me for a while that you are child again—a little boy or girl—perhaps three or four years old. Your family lives in a rustic cabin in a large forested wilderness.

A little cove of water with its sandy, gently sloping beach is just yards from your cabin beneath the trees. The perfect place for a child to play. Can you see it? The waves on the water are always tiny ones, hardly more than friendly ripples that rock your fleet of fir-cone sailboats. The sand is just the right sort for building castles and kingdoms.

It's your private world. Safe and secure. To be seen and touched and listened to as the wind whistles softly through the branches overhead. And at night you're lulled to sleep by the gentle lapping of the water along the shore.

The happy years go by and you reach that grand and adventurous age of eight. Though you still enjoy your cove, paddling just so far along its edges in a little raft, something else has captivated your imagination. It's that big mountain sloping up behind your cabin. (Daddy calls it a "hill," but you know he's wrong.)

What would it feel like to reach the top, higher than you've ever been before? To stand and look over the whole world?

Finally, that day comes, one beautiful September morning. Mom has said "Yes," and with the lunch she made packed in your small knapsack you set off on the most glorious adventure of your life—all by yourself.

Soon the cove and cabin disappear as you hike up through the woods. Sometimes you find trails to follow, sometimes you make your own, but all the while you're climbing higher and higher. Finally, after what has seemed to be hours, you break out of the trees and scamper over some rocks. In moments you find yourself standing just where you dreamed you would.

And what's the first thing you do? You turn around and look for home. There, off in the distance below, you see the sun sparkling on your little cove. But how small it is! Just up from the water, a wispy bit of smoke curls up through the trees. Home! Your little world—it's all there.

Then, looking more carefully, you see something you've never seen: Your little cove is not quite the way it has always appeared—just a little lake. Instead it's the end of a long, long neck of water that twists through the mountains until you can't see it anymore. Oh, you always knew that. But now as you actually *see* it, you realize with a start that your little world is connected to something far greater than you had ever understood.

Hours later, safely at home, you walk down to the cove after supper.

"Well, little cove," you say, "you're everything you ever were. Yet you're not the same. You're part of something very, very big."

Somehow, though everything is just like it was when you got out of bed that morning, you feel different inside. That night the sleepy lapping of the moonlit water seems to whisper deeper, wider things than it's ever whispered before.

More years go by. You're a teenager now, almost through high school. Often you've looked at a far-off snow-capped peak that dwarfs the "hill" (you now call it that too) in the foreground. Your dream—for years—has been to one day stand at the top of that soaring mountain.

Against their better judgment, your parents finally give you permission to attempt a solo climb up that proud, distant slope. That night you tremble with excitement as you collect your gear. Those rugged boots you saved to buy. Crampons, ice axe, and snow shovel, tightly stuffed mummy bag, freeze-dried food. Practice climbs are behind you now. Tomorrow you leave.

Awakening before dawn, you're halfway up the hill behind the cabin as the first sunlight spills through the trees. (Could it really have taken you half a day to climb that when you were little?) By the end of the second day you reach the base of the peak. That night the Milky Way seems brighter than you've ever seen it.

The third day, pushing hard, you set up camp just below snow level. That night you curl up snug in your snow cave—just a few hours from the top. Excitement fights long and hard against exhaustion, but finally loses in dreamless sleep.

While snow cliffs and jagged rocks are still but silhouettes against the sky, you are up and on your way. Hardly an hour after the sun has cleared the horizon, with one last surge you are there! Standing on top of the world.

Without thinking, you do exactly what you had done as a little child on another pinnacle of your life. You look for home. Searching through your binoculars, you find the winding neck of water and follow it back to where it begins—your little cove and home.

"There it is!"

Then, with your binoculars, you follow the fiord—that meandering ribbon of water—back the other way, past the mountains that had blocked your view from the hilltop years before, far off in the distant haze. Yes, you knew what you would see. And now you see it.

The vast sweep of the ocean!

Long ago you had learned why the water in your tiny cove rose and fell with the passing of the hours. It was responding to something great and far away.

"Do you mean when I was just a kid and dipped my bucket into the cove—that miles away the whole ocean moved to fill the hole I left in the water? That when I ran back and forth with my little splashing buckets attempting to fill the moat around my sand castle, the entire ocean was responding to my need?"

A few days later you find yourself once more kneeling down on the small beach. You can almost see a little child there in front of you building one more pinnacle on a castle wall. That was a special world you lived in back then. And it still is. It's all still there. But behind the cove and beyond the deep twisting fiord is fullness . . . vastness . . . almost infinity.

Christian friend, it is the same for you and me.

It's not that what we learned about God when we were children was wrong. It simply wasn't enough. Yes,

Jesus loves me, this I know, For the Bible tells me so

was true then and true now. But the scope—the wonder of that love! Have we climbed any higher? Have we seen any farther?

"Taste and See"

No matter how long any of us have walked with God, we—all of us—are still beginners. We are still at the edge of mystery. Dare we imagine what lies ahead of us—today, this week—as we climb higher and see farther into the greatness, the wonder of this magnificent God—this God who has invited us to call Him "Father"?

How tragic for us if we allow the "eyes of our heart" to become dull and nearsighted. What unspeakable loss to allow the Christian life to become a boring, passive thing as the years go by. So many of us have seemed content to paddle around the edges of that comfortable little cove of understanding we've had all our lives. Building our castles in the sand—dipping our toy buckets in the shallows—as though there were nothing more about God waiting to be discovered.

"The attributes of God? Oh, I learned all about that years ago. Heard it in a sermon series—memorized some definitions for a class in Bible college—covered it at a seminar. I don't need to go over that material again. I'm ready for something new. And anyway, if the Bible says 'How unsearchable are His judgments' and 'My thoughts are higher than your thoughts' then what's the point of spending time trying to know what is unknowable? Why don't we just accept the fact that God is all those things the Bible says He is and then get on with something we can understand? How can I possibly comprehend an incomprehensible God?"

Let me ask you another question—one that may strike you for a moment as irrelevant.

How do you define a peach?

To someone who had never seen or heard of a peach, what would you say so he would comprehend what a peach is?

"Well," you say, "it's about, ummm, three or four inches in diameter. Kind of roundish oval. Fuzzy outside. Big seed in the middle. Reddish, yellowish, orangish skin. Yellow-red meat inside, sweet and tart, juicy and firm all at the same time. A pungent, unmistakable fragrance. Biting into one on a lazy afternoon in late summer is one of life's unique pleasures."

Have you defined a peach? Not really. You could give a chemical analysis. A spectroscopic definition of its color densities. Would that do it? No! There is something about a peach that transcends anything you could ever say about it. A peach must be . . . experienced.

That is precisely what the Bible says about our relationship with God.

It says, *"O taste and see that the LORD is good"* (Psalm 34:8).

It invites us, "Come, all you who are thirsty, come to the waters . . . come, buy and eat! . . . Listen to me, and eat what is good, and your soul will delight in the richest of fare" (Isaiah 55:1-2 NIV).

God, who is aware of the infinity of His person and the impossibility of my ever being able to comprehend or describe or define Him, says, *"Come taste Me!* Just taste Me, My son, My daughter. You'll see that I am good. And once you taste Me, you're not going to worry about definitions quite so much anymore."

Once you have tasted something of the mystery of the greatness of God, the central issue is no longer "definition." The central issue becomes *response*.

How Do I Taste God?

But how does one go about "tasting" God?

Our greatest hindrance to this experience may be the pace at which we live our lives. We've been programmed to feel we can't slow down long enough to allow anything to sink in deeply. Something else incessantly clamors for our attention.

Hardly a day—hardly an hour—goes by that if we paused to think through what was happening, we would discover something more about our God. For "in Him we live and move and have our being." He is always ours to taste, to discover.

It is so easy to forget that God saved us above all else for love, for intimacy in relationship, for response. To fail to have time for *this* is to fail at living. Certainly His intentions are that everything else—service, witnessing, practical holiness—be a byproduct of our love for Him. And nurturing love takes time. Where did we ever get the idea that it simply "happens"? It doesn't.

So you take time daily for Bible reading and prayer. Fine. But how about time to mull over, to meditate, to wrestle through some of those disturbing "Whys" that most of us have about God . . . until those "Whys" dissolve into wonder and worship? What about slowing down long enough to talk to God about God? And at other times, simply to enjoy the sheer pleasure of His love? Of His forgiveness? Of His faithfulness?

One of the toughest things you and I confront is to get our thoughts off ourselves and the earth-oriented things that surround us long enough to "taste and see that the Lord is good."

And in those pressure times . . . is your only prayer, "Lord, get me out of this!"? Perhaps the main reason God allows those times is to press you closer to Himself. There is yet so much to discover about Him! And it so happens that many of our discoveries come only after those heavy, hurting struggles up the steep sides of an obstacle that often seems to make no sense at all. Finally at the top, if we're not careful, we'll slide down the far side with a sigh of relief, without first pausing to drink in the view from the top.

I am sure the apostle Paul hurt deeply as he described to Timothy the worst failure of his whole life. Not only had Paul sinned, but his sin was of the worst sort imaginable. He had poured his life into destroying the early followers of Jesus—men and women, young and old. Yet in the midst of that hurt Paul paused to relish his forgiving God. And out of that mountaintop moment comes one of the greatest doxologies ever penned.

> Now to the King eternal, immortal, invisible, the only God, be honor and glory for ever and ever. Amen. (1 Timothy 1:17)

There are doxologies yet to be penned that only you can write. What will the view be like from the top of the mountain that confronts you today? Will you pause long enough to see? To relish?

What Happened to the Beauty?

When I was in high school I went with my parents on a vacation trip through southwestern Canada. Traveling east toward Banff and Jasper Parks, we arrived at the town of Revelstoke. On our map we could see that a large national park—Glacier National Park—was just a short distance beyond. But to our disappointment we discovered there was no road through the park. The only route east was "the big bend," a long, dusty gravel road following the Columbia River as it arched northward before turning south and east to the town of Golden.

Many summers later I took my own family—Mary Jo and our two children—on the same trip. By this time the Canadian government had built a divided highway right through that mountainous park. With great expectation and a full tank of gas, we headed east out of Revelstoke ready and eager to drink in all the glory of this glacial masterpiece.

Determined to have enough time to really see it, we sped along the highway with all eyes glued to the sides of the road to watch for the first signs that we were entering the park. On and on we went. Yes, we were on the right road, but where were the signs? Where was the ranger's check-in station? From time to time we stole hasty glances at the beautiful scenery, but mostly we watched the road, looking for some clue that the park was near.

Finally, after what seemed hours, I happened to look back and noticed a sign on the *far* side of the highway that read "You are now entering Glacier National Park." We were already through it! And now it was too late to turn back. Somehow, we had missed it all—the viewpoints, the pictures we planned to take, the sidetrips we hoped to make, the massive hanging glacial cliffs we would never see. Though we could all say "We've been through Canada's Glacier National Park," we would have to add, "but we never saw it."

If you have received Jesus as your Savior and Lord, you are on the right road. But it is tragically possible you will become so occupied with the fast lane and simply getting through, that you may miss all those places where you should have slowed down—all the viewpoints, the vast panoramas of the greatness of God that

could not have been enjoyed without pausing long enough to see
. . . to taste.

Discovering God is a journey beyond all others, an adventure
that soars above our highest thoughts and kindles our deepest longings. Let's journey together, shall we?

Since this adventure is forever, the book you hold in your hands
will point out but a very few of the scenic wonders of His greatness
along the way. Yet we may find ourselves thirsting for more . . .
hungering for all the tomorrows of discovery He has waiting for
us. Perhaps we will find ourselves dreaming of those glorified bodies
we will have someday, bodies that will never weary of wonder, eyes
that will—at last—see Him as He is.

Chapter 2

Walking in His Power

I suppose every boy dreams of being connected to something bigger and more powerful than himself. Something that throbs with raw power. For some it might be the dream of rolling down the highway high in the cab of an eighteen-wheeler, or passing under the checkered flag at the Indianapolis 500.

For me, it was something else.

Every year on our ranch in Southern California, some sixty acres of citrus trees had to be sprayed with pesticide. To do it, we used a ponderous, antiquated spray rig pulled by my dad's team of huge, black Missouri mules. One person stood on top of a high tower on the rig to drive the mules and also spray the treetops. Two other men walked alongside pulling long, high-pressure hoses for spraying the sides of the trees. Since I wasn't strong enough to handle the hoses, my dad assigned me to the tower—which was just where I wanted to be.

And what a place to be! Riding on massive iron wheels far below me, the engine throbbed as it built up pressure in the pumps, drawing spray mix from the gigantic tank. Out in front, at the end of long leather reins, those big mules waited for me to command their obedience. Feeling like some lofty charioteer, I would look down over rows of trees, across the terraced hills all the way to the Pacific Ocean some ten miles away.

With the snap of the reins, I would shout "Gee-haw!" in my most gravelly voice, and watch as every sinew on the shiny wet backs of those mules began to ripple and flex. Haunches lowered, their muscular legs leaned into the load and dug deep into the soft soil. I could almost hear an "aaaahhhrrrggg" from those mules as the great wheels made a convulsive lurch and began to roll across the ground.

What a feeling to be a part of that!

Toward the end of the day, however, being responsible for all that power got a bit scary. Parts of the orchards clung to terraces overlooking the barns in the valley below. The mules, of course, knew perfectly well when it was close to quitting time, not to mention feeding time. Now and then I'd see them lift their heads and look eagerly down through the tree rows—down the terraces—at those barns. Had I let them take a shortcut, they would have catapulted me halfway down the valley.

Then one year my dad bought a Caterpillar tractor . . . and I forgot all about the mules. *Talk about power.* To me, there was nothing like sitting behind the sticks of that great machine. Sometimes working late on cold evenings, dragging a disk over the hills, I would bask in the warm waves of enveloping air blown back by the huge engine's fan. There was an almost romantic security being joined to something so powerful.

The best time of all, when my dad wasn't looking, was to ram the Caterpillar into gear and climb straight up those terraced hillsides. With its engine wide open, the tractor would claw its way up the side of the steep terrace, teeter for a moment as though it would tip over on itself, and then crash down on the level ground as it gathered RPM's to charge straight up the next one. And then up and up and up.

I shudder to think now of how many terraces I may have torn apart. But that was power! Power that moved and surged and belched clouds of smoke and dust at my command.

And I was part of it.

The Word of His Power

It was these notions of power that formed my early concepts of God's power. I could imagine Him ramming the universe into being with a mighty shove. As though God put everything He had into it, and went *"Unnnnnnhhhhhhhh!"*, and there it was! Power to me was the expenditure of energy. As though when He was through God might have sighed a long "Whew!"

But as I read the Bible more carefully I discovered something quite different. In the first chapter of Genesis, a passage describing creation, I was impressed with the fact that the emphasis was not so much on God's energy, but simply on His *words*.

> Then God said, "Let there be light"; and there was light. (1:3)
> Then God said . . . and it was so. (1:9)
> Then God said . . . and it was so. (1:11)
> Then God said . . . and it was so. (1:14-15)

If that were not clear enough, I read in Psalm 33,

> By the word of the LORD the heavens were made,
> And by the breath of His mouth all their host. (33:6)
>
> For He spoke, and it was done;
> He commanded, and it stood fast. (33:9)

Then on the seventh day, when we're told that God "rested," it wasn't from weariness at all.

> Have you not heard?
> The Everlasting God, the LORD, the Creator of the
> ends of the earth
> Does not become weary or tired.
>
> (Isaiah 40:28)

It wasn't like slumping down in a lawn chair, jerking off your work gloves, and grabbing an iced tea after mowing the lawn.

No, He just stopped speaking. That's all.

And when we finally come to the closing curtain of history, after all the ages in which God has been "upholding all things by the word of His power" (NKJV) . . . when Jesus returns to the earth in inexpressible majesty, and we hear the great shout, "Hallelujah! For the Lord our God, the Almighty, reigns!" . . . at the end of all time . . . God will still be undiminished. Still all powerful. Not tired at all.

By the *mere exercise of His will, God produces whatever He wills.* That's omnipotence.

The Whisper of His Power

But it's so hard for us to change the way we have thought. I imagined the voice of God in creation must have been at least a great cosmic shout reverberating across the universe. But no. Job, after describing God's creative acts with the words,

> He spreads out the northern skies over empty space;
>> he suspends the earth over nothing . . .

then says,

> And these are but the outer fringe of his works;
>> how faint *the whisper* we hear of him!
>> Who then can understand *the thunder* of His power?
>>> (Job 26:7 and 26:14 NIV)

I thought to myself, *If all we can see in creation is a product of God's whisper, what would happen if God ROARED?*

God has privileged you and me to live in an age where humankind is able to peer far into the heavens and probe the secrets of deep space—secrets of appalling darkness and blinding light and impossible distance. How much did Job really understand about the movements and mysteries of the planets and stars? How much did David comprehend when he wrote these lines?

> When I consider Thy heavens, the work of Thy fingers,
> The moon and the stars, which Thou hast ordained . . .
>> (Psalm 8:3)

How much did these ancient men and women of Scripture grasp about the awesomeness of the universe? We don't know. Yet we do know that God has given *this* generation the opportunity to consider His heavens as no other generation in all of time.

I was fascinated some time ago by an astronomy journal account about two stars far to the left of the "belt" in the constellation Orion. Though only one star is seen (Procyon is its name), astronomers using elaborate calculations had determined that this star has a tiny twin. By measuring their movements and the distance between these twin stars, they estimated that the smaller star was so compressed, so compacted with power, that a single cubic inch would weigh one hundred tons. Two hundred thousand pounds. Imagine dropping that on your toe!

More recently they have discovered such compression is nothing in comparison to what happens when an entire star explodes. In moments, energy is spewed out equal to that of a billion suns, producing what is called a supernova. At the same time, the star collapses in upon itself to produce a small new star . . . a neutron star. Scientists believe these mysterious objects are so compressed that a single cubic centimeter (that's less than a half-inch cube) could weigh at least a hundred billion tons. Maybe a trillion! Some become so dense that the pull of their gravity will not even allow light waves to escape. We call these black holes.

And Job says, "That is God's whisper."

"Is Anything Too Hard for Me?"

Time and again in my life I have wondered if God was "able" to do something I wanted. I assumed God could handle small things—things I could figure out. But the big things . . . the impossible things . . . that would be asking too much.

It's strange that even when we acknowledge that God has no limits, we still think in terms of "hard things" or "easy things" for which to pray.

Jeremiah wrestled with this question during the dark and dying days of his nation, Judah. Fear and famine consumed Jerusalem from within; Babylonian battering rams and assault towers pressed the siege from without. Despair draped the city streets like a dense fog . . . like a shroud. The prophet himself remained as a prisoner in the royal palace, under conviction of treason (see Jeremiah 32).

At this most inopportune moment, God commanded Jeremiah to purchase a piece of real estate from his nephew. The prophet, who had learned to be obedient to his Lord, immediately complied. He gathered the necessary witnesses, signed the deeds, and handed over the purchase price. But what must have been going on in the back of his mind? The land in question was most likely located in the middle of the Babylonian encampment. God Himself had told the prophet that the Babylonians would conquer the city and burn it to ashes. What a time to speculate in real estate! It was only too obvious that there was no value to the land. There was no logical reason to buy it. It was money down the drain! Yet when God said

"Buy it," Jeremiah reached for his checkbook.

After the transaction had been duly witnessed, notarized, and sealed, Jeremiah was left alone with the Lord.

"Ah, Lord God!" he prayed, "Behold You have made the heavens and the earth by Your great power and outstretched arm. There is nothing too hard for You" (Jeremiah 32:17 NKJV). Still on his knees, the prophet began reminding God of all the great and powerful things He had accomplished throughout Israel's history, right up to their present crisis.

We might assume that a prayer begun with such confidence would end in praise. But it doesn't. Instead, we find Jeremiah voicing doubts, coming back to the matter of the newly purchased field. The whole affair must have been tremendously baffling to him. Paraphrasing a bit, his prayer ended something like this: "Lord, umm, do You know what You asked me to do? You asked me to buy that piece of land . . . and I did, but . . . well, Lord, nothing is too hard for You . . . but . . ."

"But what, Jeremiah? *Is* anything too hard for Me? Someday I will gather My people and bring them back to this place and make them dwell in safety. And they shall be My people, and I will be their God . . . and I will faithfully plant them in this land with all My heart and with all My soul" (see 32:27 and 32:37-41).

For Jeremiah—and for us—the critical issue is never God's strength, or capacity, or ability. The issue is His *will*. By the mere exercise of His *will* He produces whatever He wills! Throughout our lives in those most perplexing, stretching times, we may rest in His power to fulfill His will. He will fulfill His promises "with all His heart and with all His soul"!

Do you remember the leper who came to Jesus? "Lord," he said, "if You are willing, You can make me clean." Jesus answered, "I am willing; be cleansed" (Matthew 8:2-3). It really is that simple.

Often we are urged by some church leaders to step out in faith. To believe God for miracles. And they are right! But if our requests (perhaps even our "demands") are based on our flesh ability to tell Him what He must do, we are really substituting our bright ideas for His, asking Him to be our slave, our genie in a bottle.

The psalmist reminds us of what happened when Israel tried to do this.

> They quickly forgot His works;
> They did not wait for His counsel . . .
> So He gave them their request,
> But sent a wasting disease among them.
>
> (Psalm 106:13-15)

"If you are willing" is a good thing to remember as we come close to God's throne in prayer.

Living in Omnipotence

Since the big issue is not God's ability, but God's will, then *to live in the will of God is to live in the omnipotence of God.* But how do we start?

For each of us there will be those times when in some mysterious way we will simply *know* that some specific thing is God's will. As we pray we may sense that we are living in His omnipotence—and we are! I doubt if Joshua gave much thought before he asked God to stop the sun. He just knew it was the right thing to do. Did he really know the complexity of what he was asking God to do? Of course not. Nor was he surprised when it happened. We might call those times the "George Mueller" moments of our lives.

But for most of us those times don't come very often. And probably it's better that way. Why? Because God's will for us—the expression of His power in us—is so much bigger than simply stopping the sun, healing our sickness, or moving mountains. In fact, it is so gigantic that no human being has ever yet comprehended its scope. The apostle Paul puts it this way:

> I bow my knees before the Father . . . that He would grant you, according to the riches of His glory, to be strengthened with power through His Spirit in the inner man; so that Christ may dwell in your hearts through faith. (Ephesians 3:14-17)

What? The omnipotent Christ—at home *inside of me?* That's right! And not only that. Paul adds,

> [that you may] know the love of Christ which surpasses knowledge, that you may be filled up to all the fullness of God. (3:19)

"The love of Christ which *surpasses* knowledge"? Impossible! "Filled up to *all* the fullness of God"? Impossible! How could God ever fill me with all of His fullness? Maybe a small part of it . . . but *all* of it? All of His love, all of His patience, all of His purity? How could even an omnipotent God do that? Yes, I know that nothing is impossible with God . . . but that is too much! It is more than I would ever dream of asking Him.

But then we read,

> Now to Him who is able to do exceeding abundantly beyond all that we ask or think, according to the power that works within us, to Him be the glory. (Ephesians 3:20-21)

"Within us!" That's right! Paul was expecting God to do something that was far, far above what I would have ever thought of imagining, much less asking. And Paul's God is my God! Dare we dream that our lives would overflow with the fullness of God's love? Yes! This is not "the impossible dream." You and I have been joined to Someone who is more powerful than we have even begun to imagine. "By the mere exercise of His will He produces whatever He wills." And He wills to fill us with Himself.

He is ready to do so. Right now. He is waiting for us to ask.

Calm at the Center of Power

A short distance east from Portland, Oregon, the vast Columbia River rolls through the majestic Columbia Gorge. Spanning that gorge is one of the great hydroelectric projects of the world, Bonneville Dam. Dozens of times on bright summer days I have driven past that dam. Once I took a tour deep inside where gigantic generators sit sedately in a long line on the polished concrete floor. I'm not sure exactly what I was expecting, but I was a little disappointed. Perhaps I was looking for something a little more dramatic. I couldn't see any movement at all! There were no thunderous roars or mechanical screams.

Just a steady rhythmic hum.

"Ah," I thought. "Maybe that's the way it is in the summer. But what about in the winter? What about when the Columbia is brown and swollen with storm water from a thousand streams?"

That thought came back to me one winter night a few years ago as I drove down the gorge during one of the worst raging storms I can remember. The icy east wind which had been blowing for two weeks had piled up massive chunks of ice in the reservoir above the dam. Tugboats kept churning the water to keep the locks from freezing solid, while millions of gallons thundered over the spillways.

Arriving home I knew that power crews would be working frantically around the clock to maintain service to the million plus people who were depending—almost for their lives—on the current coming into their homes. From time to time ice-laden wires in my neighborhood would snap, exploding nearby transformers in bursts of eerie, blue lightning. It was a most dramatic, suspenseful night.

But way up the river . . . what was it like deep in the concrete bowels of Bonneville Dam, down where the generators were? Was it dramatic and suspenseful there? No. Not a bit. Even at the peak of the storm I was sure the long line of generators would look like contented, humming, oriental monarchs seated on their pillows. They were made for this. No stress, no strain, no frantic scurrying about. By all appearances, it could have been a calm summer morning.

Over the years I've thought often of that night, especially during those times of my own inner storms . . . nights when I could not sleep . . . nights when churning clouds of problems seemed too big to handle . . . nights when surging fears drenched all hope. How could God possibly dispel the darkness? How could I possibly lift up to Him such big, impossible prayers? "Trust Him!" But why? I hadn't the faintest idea how He could ever bring me through such wild, throbbing storms. And so I would cry out again and again, "O my Father, my Father! I'm frightened and I don't even know what to ask!"

If only in times such as these you and I could pause long enough to imagine ourselves at the power source—the throne room of our omnipotent God. What would we see? No stress, no strain, no frantic scurrying about there. We would see that all is well. God was "made" for this! If only in the midst of those turbulent hours we could remember:

This hope we have as an anchor of the soul, a hope both sure and steadfast and one which enters within the veil [God's throne room]. (Hebrews 6:19)

Even when life becomes so confusing that we don't know what to say to God, His Spirit intercedes for us "according to the *will* of God" (Romans 8:27). And to live in the *will* of God is to live in His omnipotence!

Somehow it would not be quite right to have lived our whole lives without ever discovering through deep crisis times the greatness of our loving God, who needs but to "speak the word" and omnipotence is ours!

Yes, we must trust Him! And as we do, He will do exactly as He says—in His time, in His way, in His will.

Chapter 3

God Is Spirit . . . and So Am I

"God is spirit" (John 4:24).

What would it be like to exist as an invisible spirit being, without a body?

For a little while, maybe, being invisible would be an adventure—at least until the novelty wore off. But the "no body" part . . . that's something else. The scarecrow in *The Wizard of Oz* said it well: "How can you think if you don't have a brain?"

Happily, God has purposed that we function best with bodies. And most of the time we would agree with Him. A body is a handy thing to have. We might well feel sorry for anyone who didn't have one. In expressing his wish to be "at home with the Lord," the apostle Paul was not too impressed with the thought of being temporarily "unclothed" (without a body) while waiting for his resurrection body (2 Corinthians 5:2-8).

Yet for God, being pure spirit is the best. Since the choice was His, we can assume He prefers it that way—and I can think of at least one reason this might be so. It certainly would seem much easier to be omnipresent if one were spirit rather than being limited by a body. Imagine if the Holy Spirit were a physical being, trying to take up His residence in each one of us!

But what does it mean for God to be spirit?

Obviously it is not something God *has*, but rather what He *is*. Since we know a spirit "does not have flesh and bones" (Jesus said that in Luke 24:39), then a spirit being must be a complete person—thinking, feeling, and choosing—minus a body. God is certainly a complete person; in fact, He is the most complete person there is! It would be ridiculous to imagine He is in any sense less than we are because He has no body.

Yet how can we hope to respond to such a Person? He is a spiritual being and we are not.

Or . . . are we?

Spiritual Personhood

Back in the days before television, my two older sisters were allowed to stay up later than I to listen to a weekly radio program called *The Lux Radio Theater*. Feeling much put upon, I pushed my bed right up next to my barely opened door. Hoping my sisters would remember to turn up the volume, I pressed my ear against the crack. One night the director, Cecil B. DeMille, announced that they were going to dramatize Dickens's *A Tale of Two Cities*.

All was well until the story came to the place where French royalty were being sent to the guillotine. With my imagination working at fever pitch, I saw it all! The blade . . . the basket . . . the severed heads! That was too much for me! Quickly closing the door and sliding deeper into bed, I pulled the covers over my head.

Why? Because I was afraid of dying? No. I knew I was a Christian and that I would go to heaven when I died. But there was one way of dying I did not like at all. It would be all right to "just up and die," or even to be hit on the head and die. But to be *beheaded*? That was the most horrible thing I could imagine. I could see it all, in ghastly technicolor. A "swish" followed by an instant "slice." And then I would bounce and roll across the floor with my body left behind. "Please dear God, any death but that one!"

For you see, I considered my head to be more "me" than all the rest of me together. It was where my brain was. I believed *my identity was in my head*.

Years later I made a long overdue discovery. I came to Jesus' words to Nicodemus in the third chapter of John's gospel.

That which is born of the flesh is flesh; and that which is born of the Spirit is *spirit*. Do not marvel that I said to you, "You must be born again."

I knew I was born again. "Then that's it!" I thought. "My truest self—my personhood—has been changed from flesh (my brain and the rest of me) to spirit! I too am a living, functioning spirit being! And if that is so—and it is—then my brain and body are no longer most deeply who I am.

My fear of beheadings dissolved in an instant. If I were to pass into heaven by way of a chopping block, I would "say" with a shout, "You *missed* me!" (Though at that moment my voice might not be working too well.) And I would be telling the truth.

As Paul put it, when we are "absent from the body" we are "at home with the Lord" (2 Corinthians 5:8). Whether we realize it or not, every time you and I walk past the casket of a believer, we are affirming the reality of spiritual personhood.

Of course it would be wrong to act as though my body were not a part of me. It is. And I am wholly responsible for what I do with my body. But as we all should know, though we are only one "self," there are various levels to our selfhood. And the deepest level—Paul calls it our "inner man"—is spirit (Romans 7:22 and 8:10; 2 Corinthians 4:16). When we were saved, this deep level was so marvelously made alive that Paul could say, "Therefore if any man is in Christ, he is a new creature." And because of this, he could also say, "from now on we recognize no man according to the flesh" (2 Corinthians 5:16-17).

Have you and I begun to know the joy of evaluating ourselves on the basis of the fact that we are in Christ and He in us? All of those flesh-level measurements of "self-worth" that have either plagued us with pride or drowned us in self-pity are sorry measurements indeed when compared to being God's new spiritual creation!

God is spirit . . . *and so are we.*

His Spirit "bears witness with our spirit that we are children of God" (Romans 8:16). But in contrast with Him and the angels, He has purposed that we best function in bodies. Down here on earth we have "soulish" bodies. (The word "natural" in 1 Corinthians 15:44 and 15:46 is actually "soulish.") In other words, we have unredeemed bodies that are linked closely with the thinking, feeling, and choosing processes of our brains. Someday we will have "spiritual" bodies—bodies that are linked closely with the thinking, feeling, and choosing processes of our spirits.

Spiritual personhood may not be so strange after all! Yet . . . I am left with a dilemma. If God exists without a body, what am I to picture when I think of Him?

What John Saw

John the apostle groped for words. And so would you.

Though the words he used were the best ones—God saw to that—he still was limited by language. How do you describe the indescribable? How do you record what you are seeing and hearing when you know it transcends all comparisons?

A simple man, John opted for a simple description.

He had just encountered a door standing open. A door into heaven. Responding to an invitation, he stepped inside. There were no preliminaries, no successive archways, no pillared halls and ascending stairs, no pauses in gilded anterooms. He had stepped directly into the throne room of the universe. And on the throne was God.

"Behold," he wrote,

> a throne was standing in heaven, and One sitting on the throne. And He who was sitting was like a jasper stone and a sardius in appearance; and there was a rainbow around the throne, like an emerald in appearance. . . . And from the throne proceed flashes of lightning and sounds and peals of thunder. And there were seven lamps of fire burning before the throne, which are the seven Spirits of God; and before the throne there was, as it were, a sea of glass like crystal. (Revelation 4:2-6)

Later he watched as "the Lamb," the Son of God, approached the throne and took a scroll out of the right hand of "Him who sat on the throne." Six hundred years before, Daniel had described a similar experience as he saw the "Son of Man" come to appear before the "Ancient of Days." (See Daniel 7.)

John was *seeing* God the *Father* on the throne. With a physical form—having a "right hand," and "sitting." Daniel was seeing Him this way as well. How could this be? Are we also to picture the Father that way?

We are used to thinking of Jesus in a physical form—a human form. And we should. Without ceasing to be God, He became a human being, with a physical body. Even now in heaven, He possesses glorified physical humanness.

But what about God the Father? We have been taught, and rightly so, that He is spirit, even as the Holy Spirit is spirit—invisible, without flesh and bones, no body at all.

Some seem to suggest our focus should be simply on Jesus. Since He has a body, it would be "okay" for us to have some sort of mental picture of Him. But the Father? Are we to even attempt forming a mental image of Him? And if we're not, why did He appear to John as an awesome figure sitting on a throne? Why did He appear to Daniel as the "Ancient of Days," with snow-white hair and garments, and a flaming throne amid a river of fire?

Willing Accommodation

Why does He include these images in His Word?

Because He wants to accommodate us in His love.

A simple illustration may help us consider this paradox from a fresh perspective.

Your phone rings in the night. You grope for the receiver, immediately fearful of why someone would call at such an hour. Confirming your worst fears, you are told that someone very special to you—in a distant city—has been in a serious automobile accident. You arrive at the hospital hours later and are told that your loved one is in the intensive care unit.

A doctor meets you in the waiting room with grim and baffling news. The hospital staff has administered all kinds of tests and—at least for the time being—they have determined that the injured person has no ability to see or hear or speak. Nor does there appear to be any sense of feeling. The only thing the tests have been able to determine is that there is most certainly brain activity—the individual may in fact be "conscious." Curiously, the only sense that seems to be left is a sense of smell.

Emotionally shattered, you realize that when you walk into that intensive care room, there will be no way for this one you love to know you are there! How lonely this person must feel. How tragic to be cut off from everyone, yet still be conscious. What can you possibly do? How can you help that person become aware of your nearness—your love? How can you touch that person's world, bridging through the loneliness, fear, and despair?

With a spark of inspiration you remember a special fragrance that person once gave you—that bottle of cologne. Back in your hotel room, you splash that fragrance on your face and hands. Will it work? Oh, it must work! And as you enter that hospital room and step toward the bed—it does! You're rewarded with a flicker of a smile, the slightest nod.

Your loved one knows you are there! And in the days that follow, though dozens of others would be in and out of the room, that smile returns whenever the fragrance you wear comes close.

Is that fragrance *you*? No, of course not. Yet you wished so deeply to make your presence known to this one you loved that you willingly accommodated yourself to the tragic limitations you encountered.

This is precisely what the Father does! He, in His infinite being, knows our fleshly limitations. ("He knows our frame, He remembers that we are dust.") He is well aware of the value we place on faces and hands, on arms and legs. No, He is not a physical being. Yet His desire that we know an intimacy of fellowship with Him is such that He willingly accommodates Himself to our limitations. How much He must desire our responses to Him!

Therefore if it helps us for Him to appear in a physical form, He simply splashes it on.

Seeing Him in Prayer

Yet there is perhaps another reason He gives us physical pictures of Himself.

Because He wants to help us focus in our prayers.

Do you "see" when you pray? It's hard *not* to see something—if only those strange squiggles that sometimes pulsate across the darkness of our closed eyes. Often I've found myself "seeing" the people for whom I am praying. At other times, when my prayers are centered on my own needs and circumstances, I "see" them on the screen of my mind. There is probably nothing wrong with visualizing such things. Yet far too many times what I have seen beckons me to forget all about praying. Instead, I find myself wandering off in my imagination wherever those mental pictures might take me.

Could it be that God has given us those vivid, colorful pictures of Himself and His throne in order that *this* would be what we see when we pray? Often I've found that such a focus has not only kept my mind from wandering, but has actually enhanced my awareness. I've found myself increasingly overwhelmed by the inexpressible privilege of a private audience with my King.

Jesus must have had this in mind when He taught His disciples to pray, "Our Father who art in heaven . . ." (Matthew 6:9). Why did He add "in heaven"? Everybody knows that. Yet since the Bible gives us several descriptions of heaven, simply saying "in heaven" should trigger our imaginations to "see" something. I believe Jesus wanted His men—and us—to take a moment to *focus* before petitioning God.

Listen to the psalmist as he prays:

Give ear, O shepherd of Israel . . .
You who dwell between the cherubim, shine forth!"
(Psalm 80:1 NKJV)

The psalmist is "seeing" as he speaks. He is adjusting his eyes to a picture of God already painted elsewhere in Scripture. God wants us to stop and realize just *where* our prayer is ascending to . . . and Who will be listening.

Yes, we must always remember never to limit Him to our mental pictures. That would be idolatry. He is infinite Spirit and as such He transcends all human imaginations. Yet He has made us to "see" with our mind's eye. And in His accommodating grace, God has given us just enough visual information to help us focus our hearts on His magnificent glory . . . to picture our Father seated on His lofty throne, with holiness and love radiating from His face.

So go right ahead. Paint your mental pictures using all the shapes and colors the Bible gives us . . . the river of life . . . the throne room . . . millions, maybe billions of angels all praising His name.

Do you see it? Do you hear them? Now step inside . . .

Do you see HIM? How majestic could anyone be? Brighter than the sun, surrounded with all the colors of the rainbow—fantastic splendor!

Wait! He is speaking!

"Don't be afraid. Come up close. I've been expecting you."

Hello, Father.

"Hello, My child."

Sometimes you will tremble as you fall to your face before Him. And sometimes, as His little child, you will come very close and discover you aren't trembling at all.

Chapter 4

Eternal God, Eternal Destiny

He stood facing them, an angry crowd of men. When He spoke, the words were measured, steady.

"My Father, whom you claim as your God, is the One who glorifies Me. Though you do not know Him, I know Him. If I said I did not, I would be a liar like you, but I do know Him and keep His word. Your Father Abraham rejoiced at the thought of seeing My day; he saw it and was glad."

They could hardly restrain their contempt for Him, this unflinching young man in peasant's garb.

"You—you are not yet fifty years old," they spluttered, "and you have seen Abraham?"

"I tell you the truth," He replied, "before Abraham was born, I AM."

The mob surged at Him, dark with rage, eyes filled with death, eager to silence this voice that spoke such blasphemy.

"I AM!"

They knew, of course, exactly what He meant. By this statement Jesus Christ identified Himself with the name of *Jehovah*, the One who is, the One who will always be what He is.

It was a declaration of His identity—and something more.

It was also a declaration of His *eternity*. He stood before them as the eternal God, the very One who had declared Himself to their fathers as "the High and Lofty One who inhabits eternity" (Isaiah 57:15 NKJV). The One of whom Moses spoke when he cried out to the assembly, "The eternal God is your refuge, and underneath are the everlasting arms"! (Deuteronomy 33:27 NKJV).

But what does this mean? Yes, He is eternal. But I am bound within a mysterious something called time. If I can't begin to understand time, how am I to relate to Someone who is beyond time?

The Eternal "Now"

Our first tendency when we reflect on the eternity of God is to think that He has "lived a long time." That He is very old. That He has been around for ages. But Scripture is saying something different. It is saying that God simply *is*. Always has been. Never had a beginning. Will never have an end. He lives unfettered by time in any sense or in any way.

With God, there is no succession of moments. There is neither future nor past. He sees everything as one eternal *now*. He can see the whole play of history—all of it—in action right now. He doesn't have to look back. He doesn't need to look ahead. He just sees it, with the end as much immediate to Him as the beginning.

That's so hard to grasp! You and I aren't wired to handle a concept like this. Our mental circuit breakers trip the moment we try to wrap our minds around it. That is because we were built to operate within a *particular succession of moments*. Anything outside of this frame of reference makes us uncomfortable.

Years ago I watched a film of a football game. Nothing unusual about that—except it was projected at such an extremely high speed that I saw the entire game in just *three minutes*. Players ricocheted up and down the field. Cheerleaders fluttered like tiny flags in a stiff breeze. The crowd boiled in the stands. Back and forth and back and forth—a blur of color—and it was over!

If you asked me, "Well, Dave, did you see the game?" I would have to answer, "Yes and no." It was all there, but I am built by God to comprehend a certain sequence of moments at a certain rate of passage. God has so ordained it. If you attempt to speed that up too fast or stretch it out too slow, I get frustrated. It loses reality for me.

It also loses emotion. I can't say I really enjoyed "seeing" the game. Where was the anticipation of a fourth down at the one-yard line? Where was that sick feeling in the pit of the stomach when the star running back went down clutching his knee? Where was the exhilaration of victory as the clock clicked down to zero? I'm not equipped to respond emotionally when such events are too compressed. I'm not able to live that way.

Yet God is. God is eternal. In the infinity of His nature, He can see all of the succession of moments of all of time. He can grasp it all in one moment. Yet He is not frustrated. He is not disturbed.

A Thousand Years Like a Day

In his later years, perhaps just a short time before his death, the apostle Peter reflected on the eternity of the Lord he loved so deeply:

> But do not let this one fact escape your notice, beloved, that with the Lord one day is as a thousand years, and a thousand years as one day. The Lord is not slow about His promise, as some count slowness. (2 Peter 3:8-9)

Imagine the implications of those words! To God, a single day could be like a thousand years of existence—and a thousand years to God could be seen as just one day. God can see all of history from the death of Christ to this very hour as only a couple of days on His calendar.

Moses captured the same thought when he prayed:

> LORD, You have been our dwelling place in all generations.
> Before the mountains were brought forth,
> Or ever You had formed the earth and the world,
> Even from everlasting to everlasting, You are God . . .
> For a thousand years in Your sight
>   are like yesterday when it is past,
>   and like a watch in the night.
>   (Psalm 90:1-4 NKJV)

Perhaps we can visualize this by placing ourselves in a spaceship hovering somewhere around two thousand light years out in space—only one-fiftieth of the way across our galaxy, the Milky Way.

Next, imagine that we have on board a telescope powerful enough to see small details on faraway planet Earth. Keep in mind that light from Earth—the scenes we will be looking at—has been traveling through space at 186,000 miles per second for two thousand years. And if somehow we could focus on just the right spot and just the right moment . . . we would find ourselves actually watching a Man bearing a cross through the narrow streets of Jerusalem. We would see Him ascend a rocky hill, just outside of town. The crucifixion of our Lord would "happen" right before our eyes.

That very moment would intersect with your spacecraft. The light that began to travel from Earth as Jesus was being nailed to the cross is even now nearly two thousand light-years out into space, still shooting out into the depths of the universe. Unchanged. Undiminished. Still bearing that awful moment for any who might find a way to behold it.

Let's stretch our imagination again by assuming our spaceship has set its course toward Earth and will make the entire trip in two days' time. If you kept your eye against the telescope lens, two thousand years of history would come tearing into your vision like water out of a firehose. You would be seeing a thousand years as a day.

You and I could not endure that. But it presents no difficulty to the eternal God. Because He is eternal, God could choose to know the utter and inexpressible joy He finds in His Son the Lord Jesus, and at the same moment could enter into the horror of that instant when His Son cried, "My God, My God, why have You forsaken Me?" Nor is He disturbed by what seems to us such an impossible paradox.

He is eternal.

A God Who Moves through Time

These thoughts raise logical—and troubling—questions. If God in His eternal nature can see everything at once, past and future, how can He truly identify with me in the moments of my life? Does He in any sense move through time with me? Or does God so live in one eternal "Now" that my failure of tomorrow is casting a shadow on His joy in me today?

We know, for instance, that the Bible says "Do not grieve the

Holy Spirit." Is God, then, grieving today because He knows you're going to sin against Him tomorrow—even though you are walking in love and thanksgiving and purity *today?* Is God saying, "Well, I see that you are seeking Me today. But I can see your whole life at the same time and know that you're going to blow it tomorrow. So I don't see your life in terms of the quality of our relationship right now—I see the whole thing. Instead of seeing today as a beautiful, sparkling white day and tomorrow a black day, all I see when I look at you is a smudgy gray"?

What an unbearable tragedy that would be! Thank God the Bible gives us ample evidence that He doesn't see us this way. There certainly are times when for one reason or another I bring grief to the Holy Spirit. But there are also times when I bring joy to His heart. God moves with me through those moments.

We can see this truth illustrated in how God led the nation of Israel across the wilderness. He moved through time with them. He shared their moments of triumph and joy. He was angered by their moments of stubborn disobedience. He looked forward with them to the joys of the promised land. He grieved when they threw that privilege away through their lack of faith.

This is a precious thing God has chosen to do. He too awaits the consummation of all things. He too looks forward to your arrival in heaven—He's waiting for it. What a moment it will be for Him!

Throughout His life on earth, Christ spoke of those things He was *looking forward to.* We learn in 1 Corinthians 15 that there will be a point in time, at the end of history, when the Lord Jesus delivers up the kingdom to the Father. All of heaven—including heaven's Lord—anticipates that moment!

Yet how can this be? How can God see the whole sweep of history at one glance and yet remain intimately involved with the mundane moments of my Monday morning?

As I've pondered these thoughts, casting about for some kind of analogy, a favorite trip of mine comes to mind. A seventy-mile length of highway winds through the Columbia River Gorge. It follows the river's march through the Cascade Mountains on its way to the Pacific. How I love that drive! Stratified cliffs tower several hundred feet above the river. Waterfalls by the dozens leap down the mountainsides. And then there is the river itself. Wide and mighty. Regal and unhurried. Each time just a little bit different. On one trip slate-gray and smooth as glass . . . the next time piercing blue, the wind making rainbows in the spray of its waves.

When friends come from out of state to visit us, it's natural that we suggest a drive up the gorge.

Since I've been over that stretch of highway so often—perhaps a hundred times—I can, in a sense, see the whole journey *at once*. I can visualize literally every bend in the road. Every sheer-faced cliff. Every thundering waterfall. Every awesome vista. I can see it all in one mental mural, from beginning to end.

Though it would be difficult to do, I could keep that picture in my mind as I travel with our friends. Around every turn I could say, "Ah yes, I see it all. Such and such is next. No surprises."

But there is a better way for me to take that trip. I can choose to experience the journey *with* them. I can choose to move through time with those dear friends who are riding as visitors along this marvelous highway.

That's much more enjoyable! So as I drive I refrain from "looking ahead." Where my eyes fall, that's where I look. I'm not thinking about the view around the bend, I'm simply enjoying what my friends are enjoying. I'm looking at what they're looking at. When they turn suddenly in their seats and say, "Oh!" I turn in my seat and say, "Oh!" I am with them—really *with* them—in the experience. Their next moment is my next moment. Their *right now* is my *right now*.

By some unfathomable mystery, God deals with us in the same way. He is *with* us in this journey of living. What an amazing and precious thing! He need not be. Yet He is. He has chosen to be. Tomorrow is tomorrow with God, yesterday is yesterday, today is today, and this moment is this moment. Therefore when you go through times of grief, you have a sympathetic God who identifies with you. And when you experience great joy, you have an empathetic High Priest who shares your delight.

He has so chosen. To move through time with us. And I think it is because He loves us so much.

A Day Like a Thousand Years

But Peter says not only that to God a thousand years is like a day; he also says that *a day is like a thousand years*.

Just for the fun of it, I recently fished out my pocket calculator to see how such a thousand-year day would break down. Each hour would last for forty-two years! Each minute calculates out to 254 days—or *eight and a half months*. Every second stretches on for 102 hours.

What would you think if the happiest moment of your life lasted not for sixty seconds, but for thirty-four weeks? A dream come true? No! Just the opposite. You would be ready for a straitjacket before the first day was over. Mentally, emotionally, and for that matter, physically, we're not built to handle such stress—even happy stress. That is because, once again, God has ordained that you and I should live within a certain sequence of moments. And stretching out those moments would be just as disconcerting to us as compressing them down. Yet to our God, thousand-year days are no problem at all.

"A single day as a thousand years" . . . what is God telling us through these words? I believe God wants us to appreciate the relative value of the moments of our life.

In the immediate context, Peter was underlining the fact that we should never force upon God our evaluation of time. Part of his perspective is that not all time is *equal* time. There may be times in our lives when a single day is in God's sight equal to a thousand years of ordinary living. Ironically, the very moments God considers most valuable, we may consider most worthless!

Within the span of our lives we find ourselves facing days of great trial, crushing grief, and bitter confrontation with the powers of darkness. How we wish those hours would pass! Our prominent prayer becomes, "Lord, *get me out of this!*"

Yet if we listen for God's reply, we might hear Him say, "Wait a minute. This very day in your life is worth a thousand years. Don't rush it!"

Think of all the years Joshua and Caleb lived. But there was one period of time, perhaps no more than an hour, that was to them and to God worth a thousand "run-of-the-mill" lifetimes. During those brief moments they stood alone before a faithless, rebellious assembly and declared that with God's help, the Israelites could face any obstacle and claim the promised land as their own. Hear the echo of their words as they ascended to that pinnacle moment of their lives:

> We should by all means go up and take possession of it, for we shall surely overcome it. . . . If the LORD is pleased with us, then He will bring us into this land, and give it to us. . . . Only do not rebel against the LORD. (Numbers 13:30 and 14:8-9)

What a hard moment it was for them! They were repudiated by their people, rejected by their fellow spies. They tore their clothes and their very hearts were torn with pain. Their people were rushing headlong into rebellion against God—judgment and wrath hovered in the air. It was an excruciating moment. A nightmare. They must have longed for it to end. But in God's sight, that one moment of courageous living was like a *lifetime* of humdrum living. Their very lives hinged on that hour!

For Queen Esther as well, there was one day when, at the peril of her life, she spoke a word before the king for the sake of her people . . . a day that was worth her whole life.

Think of Stephen. How many "average" days did he experience in his lifetime? How many normal tasks had he performed between the rising and setting suns? But there was *one day* . . . a day when Stephen, preaching his heart out, met a wall of hate and a hail of stones. "Look," he said, "I see heaven open and the Son of Man standing at the right hand of God!" Yelling at the top of their voices, an enraged mob rushed him out of the city and began smashing his body with every rock they could grab. Broken and dying, he slumped to the ground and said, "Lord, do not hold this sin against them."

One day . . . hardly more than a few minutes. Yet in God's eyes that day was worth a lifetime. If that had been the only day Stephen had lived, in God's sight it was as a thousand years.

Consider Job. God had sorted through all the human race, picked one man, held him out, and said, "Satan, watch this man!" Then, within a comparatively brief period of his life, this godly man went through adversities of unbelievable proportions. As wave after wave of pain and horror thundered over him, Job must have felt as though his life was slipping away—like sand through his fingers. Even his wife urged him to "curse God and die."

Yet at that moment, when he saw his life as less than worthless, time was standing still and all heaven (except God) was holding its breath. Moments which to Job held no meaning at all had gained value beyond his wildest imaginations. How could he have known that God had chosen him to be "Exhibit A" before all the principalities and powers of the universe? Here was a man who would not blaspheme his God, *no matter what*.

And there were others.

Abraham . . . on that darkest of nights before that early morning when he left with Isaac for Mount Moriah.

Peter . . . as he took that first step on the stormy Sea of Galilee.

David . . . as he picked up those five smooth stones in the Valley of Elah.

The whole of Hebrews 11 . . . men and women confronting crossroads of destiny . . . days, minutes, *seconds* worth a thousand years.

When were these people most fully alive? For many, it was when life seemed most threatened—when life by all appearances was being lost.

No, all time is not of equal worth. So often in those deep testing periods in each of our lives, in those harsh, sunless days of disappointment and hurt and shattered plans, we feel as though life is slipping away from us. We feel that hopes and dreams are scattering like leaves in a November wind. Perhaps for one reason or another our lives end up being shorter than we expected, and the sand slips through the hourglass faster than it was ever supposed to.

We cry out, "Lord! I'm *losing* it!" God answers, "Oh no, My child. These moments of trust and submission are more precious to Me than hours or weeks of plain existing. I am making a day for you like a thousand years of living. These are your moments of fullest life!"

"But for a Moment . . ."

Perhaps at this very moment—even as you read these words—you are hurting because you feel you are missing out on life. You feel loneliness while others seem surrounded with close friends . . . disablement while others are so robust . . . rejection while others receive praise . . . unceasing physical pain while those who visit you relax in comfort.

"It isn't fair!" you find yourself thinking. "Why have days slipped by that could have been so full of happiness? What have I done to deserve this?"

If only you and I could more quickly catch a glimpse of God's eternal perspective in such times of trial and suffering. But that's not an easy thing to do. God is asking us who live in time to recognize a perspective of existence that none of us has ever yet experienced—an eternal perspective. The apostle Paul presses this when he writes,

> . . . our light affliction, which is but for a moment, is working for us a far more exceeding and eternal weight of glory. (2 Corinthians 4:17 NKJV)

When we look at the apostle's life, those words are a little hard to swallow. Wasn't this the same man who had been pursued like a criminal from town to town? Wasn't this the same man who had been stoned and left for dead, beaten and flogged repeatedly, shipwrecked, maligned, humiliated? What about those long, weary weeks of imprisonment in dank dungeons? What about the heart-wrenching rejection he suffered from other Christians—the very ones he had dedicated his life to love and serve? Wasn't he the one who took up the pen with a manacled hand and wrote, "Everyone in the province of Asia has deserted me . . ."?

Yet Paul could write of his *"light* affliction." Was he being cynical? His afflictions weren't light at all! They were terribly heavy. "Come on, Paul. You're joking! I would have crumbled if I had to live through the things you faced. What do you mean, 'our light affliction'?"

"When you weigh your troubles," Paul would tell us, "it all depends on what you place on the opposite side of the scales." Put all your heartaches and losses and disappointments on one side.

They will seem unbearably heavy until you place "the eternal weight of glory" on the other side. Suddenly "heavy" becomes "light" when weighed against such eternal delight.

> Therefore we do not lose heart, but though our outer man is decaying, yet our inner man is being renewed day by day. For momentary, light affliction is producing for us an eternal weight of glory far beyond all comparison, while we look not at the things which are seen, but at the things which are not seen; for the things which are seen are temporal, but the things which are not seen are eternal. (2 Corinthians 4:16-18)

But Paul . . . that's so hard to do! Maybe if our suffering came as a result of faithfulness in witnessing—real persecution for the gospel's sake—maybe in a circumstance like that we could "focus on the unseen." But so much that is heavy is just a part of living. Circumstances press in upon us. The cravings of our flesh seem so insistent and immediate. On top of all that, our enemy battles in the craftiest ways to steal God's eternal perspective from us. He seems to know each of our special weaknesses.

If we sat down together, you and I could relate story after story of Christian couples whose lives and ministries have been blasted by marital unfaithfulness. Choice young couples who stepped out to serve the Lord with great expectation and then—perhaps because of unfulfilled desires, an insensitive spouse, an attractive associate, a compromising circumstance—their marriage, their witness, and their relationship with God all lie shattered.

I remember sitting in a coffee shop across the table from a dear friend of mine. She talked to me about her loneliness, about a husband who seemed calloused to her needs, and about her new lover . . . a man who filled those empty spaces, a man who satisfied all those deep wholesome human longings she felt.

I pleaded with her to change the direction she was moving. Praying silently, fervently, I told her that what she was doing was blatant sin. There was no justifying it. No rationalizing. No twisting the words to somehow make it right. It wasn't gray, it was dead black, and it would grieve the heart of God.

"But David," she said, "if I miss this, I'll miss what I have dreamed of all my life. How can I keep going on with things as they are? Yes, I know it's wrong. But don't you understand? Why can't you see? This is too important. I can't go back on it now. This is what I want!"

As if to soften the raw edge of her rebellion against God, she then quoted (completely out of context), "And we know that God causes all things to work together for good," (carefully stopping short of the words "to those who love God").

"No, this won't work out for good," I told her. "And whatever suffering or disappointment you might experience by saying 'No' to the desires of your flesh—no matter how painful—is *nothing* alongside eternity."

I could not tell her that her husband would become the man she wanted him to be. Perhaps he would . . . perhaps he never would. Perhaps for the rest of her life she would have to face those shattered expectations—those long, barren days of loneliness. Perhaps for the rest of her life she would have to live with a man who seemed as cold as a fish and as hard and unresponsive as a rock. I don't think that would have been the case, but it makes no difference. Somehow the brief, fleeting span of years that lay before her had become everything—life itself.

May God teach us that this is not so!

You may find yourself confronted with a temptation toward sin that seems to be such a demanding, incessant, irresistible thing that you feel yourself falling and don't know how to stop. You may begin to think, "To say no to this is more than anybody ought to ask of a human being—it's more than God ought to ask!"

Yet in light of our eternal destiny, God would say to us that it would be better to go crazy than to succumb to such a sin. It would be better to end up in a mental institution, scraping your nails against a padded cell, than to break the law of God! *Anything* is better. You are His royal child. Your destiny is eternal glory. God has said that you are more than a conqueror through Jesus Christ—no matter how intense the pressure, no matter how attractive the temptation. Dare we frustrate God's eternal purposes?

For all of us there will come emotional pains which will be more difficult to bear than almost any physical pain. But Paul would remind us that these periods of pain are temporary—"but for a moment." He would also tell us that "the sufferings of this present time are not worthy to be compared with the glory which shall be revealed in us" (Romans 8:18 NKJV).

Our sufferings are not even worth comparing with heaven! In other words, it isn't even a fair contrast to say, "Well, I've got this problem and that problem . . . but just think, someday I'm going to have heaven!"

Paul says the comparison isn't worth mentioning. There is *no* comparison! "Eye has not seen, nor ear heard, nor have entered into the heart of man the things which God has prepared for those who love Him. But God has revealed them to us through His Spirit" (1 Corinthians 2:9-10 NKJV).

He *has* revealed these things. But we must open the eyes of our heart to see them.

We'll Never Die!

One last fact about eternity can help in our struggle to see life from God's perspective: We who are His *are never going to die*. For us, eternity *has already* begun. We received eternal life the moment we trusted Jesus as our Savior and Lord. In that instant, we became alive to God. And because of it, you and I will never die.

It's understandable—and, for that matter, biblically accurate—to say that a believer who has gone to be with the Lord *has died*. But it is accurate only in the sense that the person's *body* has died. In fact it is interesting to note how cautious the New Testament is in speaking of Christians "dying." Remember what Jesus said about Lazarus? "Our friend Lazarus has fallen asleep" (John 11:11). Later, however, because His disciples thought He was speaking of literal sleep, He said, "Lazarus is dead."

More often than not, Paul also spoke of loved ones who had died as having "fallen asleep." Even when he spoke of his own imminent passing, he never said, "Listen, disciples, I'm going to die!" In his last letter to Timothy, his dear son in the faith, Paul wrote, "The time of my departure has come" (2 Timothy 4:6). It wasn't the idea that he was going to die, but that he was going to God!

Peter, too, facing his inevitable execution at the hands of the Romans, spoke of "the tent of this body," and said, "I know that I will soon put it aside" (2 Peter 1:13-14 NIV).

He wasn't going to die—just move to another tent!

You and I will never die. Not really. Jesus said to Martha, "He who believes in me will live, even though he dies; and whoever lives and believes in me will never die" (John 11:25-26 NIV).

It's true! You and I, if we belong to Jesus, will never die. Yes, we will, perhaps, know the difficulties and the pains of our *mortality's* death. And that hurt of mortal death is a real hurt, a real enemy. But we—the real you, the real me—will never taste death. When the Lord calls us home, we'll shed these mortal bodies, "for this corruptible must put on incorruption, and this mortal must put on immortality. . . . Death is swallowed up in victory" (1 Corinthians 15:53-54 NKJV).

We will never die.

Such a delicious thought! I think God wants us to relish the fact that we will live forever.

As a matter of fact, we're not even getting old. "Oh, yes I am!" you answer. "I looked in the mirror this morning." But no. *You* are not getting old. Oh sure, your mortality is getting old, the old tent has some lines and wrinkles and signs of wear . . . but so what? What is that alongside the dominant, unshakable reality of eternal youth?

A number of years ago our family was camping in a great redwood forest on the Oregon-California border. I went for a walk one morning among those massive trees, some nearly two thousand years old. As I walked I couldn't help thinking how short my life was. What would it be? Seventy, eighty, maybe ninety years at the most.

I can remember thinking, *It's not fair, Lord!* I looked at those solemn, towering giants and thought, *You're going to be lifting your branches to the blue sky when I'm rotting in a grave. Certainly a human being ought to live longer than a tree.* Hadn't God mixed up His priorities somehow?

Then I laughed. *David, you dumb jerk. Long after this tree has fallen into dust you'll still be young—tasting forever of the tree of life.*

I'm going to be young forever! What an inexpressible joy! To be God's new creation . . . built for eternity . . . His workmanship. And while we live here on earth He is using time—that sometimes painful sequence of moments—to add facets to that spiritual diamond that is me, so that I'll be able to more perfectly reflect His beauty and glory throughout eternity. What a precious process that is!

Finally, when He thinks I am ready, He'll take that diamond to heaven to flash and sparkle forever—not in itself, but in the reflected light of the glory of our eternal God.

But Won't We Get Bored?

There is one thing about this mystery of our living forever that could cast a shadow on the pure pleasure God wishes us to find when we think about our own endlessness. It has to do with the question, "Forever is such a long time. Won't we get bored in heaven?" This question is especially relevant for us in the Western world because we are far more *time* conscious than *event* conscious.

Let's think about this for a moment. Can you remember an event in your life when your consciousness of the event so dominated your thoughts that there was no room for time consciousness to interfere? Time has been ruling most of us for so long we have to think way back to childhood to find such an event. Perhaps it was building a sand castle at the beach, or a tree house in the backyard or shooting baskets with friends. "Come in and clean up for dinner!" your mom called. "I'm coming!" you answered. And you meant it. But the event swallowed up your words. It was simply too consuming for time to gain control.

We become conscious of the passing of time only when something causes us to turn our thoughts away from *what* we are doing to consider *how long* we have been doing it. Those "somethings" could include fatigue—mental, emotional, or physical. Or other duties and deadlines. Or maybe the event wasn't all that exciting to begin with.

Happily, all those "somethings" will someday be vaporized by our infinitely creative God, plus the resources of our future glorified bodies. Nothing will ever cause us to turn away from the glory to consider how long we've been there. There's not a chance for boredom! Can you imagine drinking in the captivating wonder of your God—and then looking down to check your watch? Time simply won't have an opportunity to interrupt.

The eternal *event* will swallow up time forever.

Chapter 5

His Face . . . toward Me

Listen. The song drifts through the darkness, across the grassy hills.

> Where can I go from Your Spirit?
> Or where can I flee from Your presence?

The singer, a silhouette merging with the blackness of the Judean hillside, lifts his face to a wide mantle of stars.

> If I ascend into heaven, You are there;
> If I make my bed in hell, behold, You are there.

Riding the hill-crests, rippling through the little valleys, a light wind carries the words far into the night.

> If I take the wings of the morning,
> And dwell in the uttermost parts of the sea,
> Even there Your hand shall lead me,
> And Your right hand shall hold me.

> If I say, "Surely the darkness shall fall on me,"
> Even the night shall be light about me;
> Indeed, the darkness shall not hide from You,
> But the night shines as the day;
> The darkness and the light are both alike to You.
>
> (Psalm 139:7-12 NKJV)

What was David saying? "Oh Lord, how shall I flee from Your Spirit—You always get there ahead of me! You move around so fast!"

No, that isn't what the awestruck songwriter had in mind at all. It isn't that God gets places fast. He is simply *there*. Wherever you go, wherever you run, wherever you hide. He is there.

"Am I a God who is near . . . and not a God far off?" the Lord asks in the book of Jeremiah. "Can a man hide himself in hiding places, so I do not see him? . . . Do I not fill the heavens and the earth?" (23:23-24).

He *fills* the heavens! He *fills* the earth!

A generation after the shepherd-king sang his wonder to the night sky, his own son ponders the same searching questions. Even as he dedicates the new temple—even as the glory of God begins to fill that temple—Solomon realizes that no earthly building can house the great King.

> But will God indeed dwell on earth? Behold, heaven and the highest heaven cannot contain Thee, how much less this house which I have built! (1 Kings 8:27)

In a sense, the Holy Spirit leads Solomon beyond what He would say to the prophet Jeremiah. To the prophet, God would say, "Jeremiah, I fill heaven and earth." But Solomon's words go further than that. God not only fills heaven and earth, but heaven and earth cannot contain Him! The highest heaven cannot contain Him!

When He created all that there is, the first chapter of Genesis tells us that "God saw." He stepped back from the universe—from His entire creation—and looked at it. And standing outside of it, looking on, He said, "That's good."

Ours is a God who is not only *immanent*, in the sense that He is totally within everything that there is, but He is also *transcendent*. If all the universe disappeared in a moment, God would still be. He is not confined within His creation. In Psalm 8, David declares that God has set His glory "*above* the heavens."

But Doesn't God Live in Heaven?

Knowing as we do that God is everywhere, isn't it a little puzzling that Jesus teaches us to pray, "Our Father, *who art in heaven . . .*"?

Why do we have to pray to Him up there? After all, He lives within me! Why can't I look down at the front of my shirt and pray, "Our Father . . ."? What's the point of focusing on heaven?

In Matthew 18:10, Jesus spoke of the angels who "continually behold the face of My Father who is in heaven." I have concluded that heaven must be that place—a place of a totally different dimension, not of this creation at all—where God has chosen to always manifest His glory.

It's not as though He's more *there* than *here*; it's just that He has chosen heaven as the place where His glory will forever be on display. The radiance, the fire of His being will always be seen by those who surround His throne.

To help us visualize this thought, imagine a very long table, running the length of a great hall. Now imagine that this entire table is piled high with a particular kind of rock. Thousands and thousands of rocks, all very similar in size and appearance. Suddenly someone turns out the lights in this cavernous hall—except for an ultraviolet light which I hold in my hand. I then decide to shine this special light on one small area of the table.

Any of you who have seen certain rocks displayed under such a light know what would happen. The rocks would flame with greens and yellows and blues and reds and oranges. The colors would seem almost to dance upon the stones. Fantastic beauty seen only with ultraviolet light.

Were those particular rocks different from the rest? Not a bit. In fact, anywhere on that table I might choose to shine that light you would see a similar display of glory. It's not in the light; it's in the rocks themselves. But I can choose where that glory will be seen.

That is a picture of heaven. Since God is everywhere, His intrinsic glory is everywhere, too. But He can choose to reveal His glory wherever He wishes. For reasons known best to Him, He has chosen a place He calls "heaven" to constantly have His magnificent glory on display. Of course, God could display the visible radiance of His glory anywhere in the universe He wished. He could display it at some point between Earth and Venus. He could display it outside your front door. But you would not be able to endure it. We simply aren't built to take it (yet), and He knows that.

God's friend Moses asked for such a display at one time, and the Lord complied—with very stringent safeguards:

Then Moses said, "Now show me your glory."

And the LORD said, "I will cause all my goodness to pass in front of you, and I will proclaim my name, the LORD, in your presence. . . . But," he said, "you cannot see my face, for no one may see me and live."

Then the LORD said, "There is a place near me where you may stand on a rock. When my glory passes by, I will put you in a cleft in the rock and cover you with my hand until I have passed by. Then I will remove my hand and you will see my back; but my face must not be seen." (Exodus 33:18-23 NIV)

God filters the brilliance of His glory . . . for our sake. But that fact should not lead us to doubt the shining reality of His presence. Wherever you are at this moment, He is there . . . in His majestic fullness. In His radiant splendor. You could not be in a more sacred spot in all the world. Not even if you journeyed to Israel to "walk where Jesus walked." Not even if you knelt in the Garden Tomb as the morning sun crested the horizon on Easter Sunday. Wherever you are—at your dining room table, in your dormitory room, in your car, at your office desk, standing at the kitchen sink, sitting in the back booth of a smoke-filled roadside diner—you are in the awesome presence of your Lord and your God.

Knowing the limits of our unredeemed mortality, He "covers us with His hand" so we are not vaporized by the blazing corona of His glory. But someday, in our redeemed bodies, bodies able to bear the unbearable wonders of heaven, *we will see Him as He is*. We will not have to hide. Isaiah 6 tells us that the mighty seraphim cover their eyes with their wings as they hover in the presence of His throne. Yet the Bible never says you and I will have to do that.

A Troubling Question

A number of years ago these thoughts about the omnipresence of God brought me to a question for which I could find no answer. I had encountered several passages in the Bible that seemed to indicate it is possible for a person to "depart from the presence of God." Yet how could that be? How can you depart from the presence of a God who is everywhere? It seems impossible. And yet Genesis 4:16 tells us:

> Then Cain went out from the presence of the LORD, and settled in the land of Nod, east of Eden.

Doesn't the Lord say He fills heaven and earth? How do you walk away from that?

In the New Testament, Paul gives us a far more comprehensive—and horrible—expression of this paradox:

> The Lord Jesus shall be revealed from heaven with His mighty angels in flaming fire, dealing out retribution to those who do not know God and to those who do not obey the gospel of our Lord Jesus. And these will pay the penalty of eternal destruction, away from the presence of the Lord and from the glory of His power. (2 Thessalonians 1:7-9)

Away from His presence? Away from His glory? How could that be?

Remember Moses' response when he wrestled with the real and terrifying possibility that God's presence would no longer accompany Israel on her journeys? Shaken to the core of his being, Moses told the Lord, "If Thy presence does not go with us, do not lead us up from here" (see Exodus 33:1-15). God had offered to send an angel ahead of the nation instead of Himself, but Israel's embattled leader would have none of it. "If Your presence doesn't come with us, God, this is where we camp. We're not going another step!"

How do such expressions coincide with the fact that God's presence is everywhere? The apparent disparity in these passages left me feeling troubled—and more than a little confused. Then one afternoon a realization burst through my perplexity like a shaft of light. I finally had an answer to the questions that had shadowed me for such a long time—an answer that opened up a new world of appreciation and awe within my heart.

Very simply, I remembered that the word *presence,* in both the Old Testament Hebrew and the New Testament Greek, is always the word for "face."

When David, therefore, was praying, "Where can I flee from Your presence," he was not only confronting the fact that God was *there,* but even more, he was reveling in the fact that *God's face was turned his way.*

"O God," David was saying, "You're not only here, but You are looking my way! You are always aware of me!"

Have you ever been in a crowd of people—perhaps in an elevator, pressed in that tiny crowded compartment—yet you felt terribly alone and lonely? There could scarcely be a more graphic example of the "omnipresence" of people. There you are in silence, shoulder to shoulder with a dozen people, all eyes watching the sequencing floor numbers. It's as though *you* don't matter at all. Their faces are not your way!

When God, therefore, speaks of His presence—His face—He is saying much more than simply that He is there. It is a term that underlines a most wonderful truth: the reality of personal relationship.

You and someone very dear to you could be sitting together on a park bench. You would be correct in saying that the other person, the bench, and you are all equally "omnipresent," equally "close." But there is a world of difference between that person and the bench!

Moses understood this when God reassured him with the words, "My presence shall go with you, and I will give you rest (Exodus 33:14). God was saying, "Moses, not only will I be there where you are, but My focus will be on you. You will be on My mind. I will never look away!"

Our home is on a hillside a few blocks from an elementary school. When our son Greg was attending the school, my wife Mary Jo occasionally would look down to the school playground to see if she could spot her little boy. It was not too difficult to pick him out among all those little bodies scurrying about. Sometimes when she looked, suddenly she would see among hundreds of children one little hand raised high, waving toward the house. Because of the glare on the windows, it was impossible for Greg to see her from the playground, but he simply assumed his mom was there and would be waving back. How often, she wondered, had he waved when she was not there?

Child of God, do we even begin to comprehend that whenever

we wave toward home, God waves back? His face is always our way!

But God does not share this relationship with everyone. His face will not be toward the one who rejects His grace and spurns His love. Cain, with willful determination, walked away from the face of God. There was no longer any relationship. And the destiny of all who reject Christ, according to 2 Thessalonians 1:9, is to ultimately be removed from the face of God . . . forever. There will be no hope of any relationship. Never, in all eternity, will God look their way again.

That is hell.

Encounter in the Moonlight

Years ago, while pastoring a church in southern California, I found myself becoming increasingly discouraged. Not with the church—I could not have asked for finer people. Certainly not with my family. And not with my surroundings, either. Our coastal resort town was a delightful place to live.

I was discouraged with myself.

Sometimes, rather than driving to work, I would walk down a few blocks from our home to the beach. There I would follow along the shoreline for a mile or so, to finally climb the steps of the sea cliff to the church, only a block from the beach. What a daily commute! But there were times upon arriving at the bottom of those steps that I had to talk myself into making the climb. Beyond those stairs was a ministry that glaringly exposed my inadequacies.

"O God," I found myself praying, "please . . . if I could only just keep walking and walking by the sea until I could not walk anymore. Why do I have to climb those steps?"

Late one night my depression seemed especially dark. Not being able to sleep, I left our home and found myself minutes later standing as close to the sea as the incoming waves would allow. In spite of myself, I could not help noticing the great orb of the full moon hanging out over the ocean. For a long time I simply looked and listened to the thunder of the surf. I noticed that sometimes when a series of huge breakers rolled in, the moonlight would dance across the phosphorescent foam, tumbling upon itself, swishing far up the sand. And then, as though spent, the sea would calm and the streak of light from the moon would lie flat with a brilliant sheen all the way across the wet sand to my feet.

"That's amazing!" I thought. "Since the sea on either side of that streak appears dark, it is as though the moon is putting on a private show for *me*. Just for me. If I step this way—the streak stays with me. And if I jump way over there—it's there, too!

Just for the fun of it, I ran down the beach. The streak of light kept right with me. It never stopped. It was never too late. It never got there before I did. It was just there—wherever I stood. It was as though the whole moon concentrated its radiance straight through the vault of space, across the vast Pacific . . . to *me*.

Then I thought to myself, "Well, David, this is what God is to you, isn't it?"

The Lord taught me through that late-night object lesson. It was as though He was saying, "David, My *face* is your way. You can run as fast as you can. You can travel as far as you like. You can hide as long as you will. My *face* will be toward you. I will never turn away."

My mind began to carry the analogy further. Sometimes the streak of moonlight exploded in the tumult of the breakers, the curling phosphoresence and backwash of the waves. At other moments the streak seemed serene and undisturbed. And God seemed to say, "David, it makes no difference what your circumstances are. Twisted and troubled like a riptide, or completely calm and at rest. It doesn't matter, David. My face is still your way. All that I am is yours to dispel the darkness."

"Lord," I found myself praying, "if that is so, the moon shows more glory when the sea is most troubled. Could it be that You are best seen in those times, too?" (I thought of the disciples in the storm.)

But what if someone had been standing right beside me at that moment? Would he or she see exactly what I was seeing? No, he or she would not. He would see his own private display of the moon's glory . . . a picture formed by the unique circumstances of those particular waves between that person and the moon.

Would my private display of moonlight be lessened if someone were standing next to me? No—not a bit. What if a million people crowded onto that shoreline, each person on his own little niche of sand, each one with his or her own private display of moonlight? Would my display be diminished? Not at all!

As I walked back home that night I rested in the mystery that my omnipresent God was also my personal God. Yes, He is everywhere, and yet His face is most personally toward each of His children. *Each* of us!

Perhaps someone reading these words at this very moment is grappling with loneliness and discouragement. Hope seems so distant, so unreachable. God's face is your way! Right now. Can you see Him? Picture the moonlight on the sea. All that God is—not just part of Him, but *all* that He is—is your way.

My Face . . . toward Him

Though one day our eyes will actually look upon His face, for now we see Him through the eyes of faith alone. And though I do not yet see Him in a visible way, my life is changed as I look and look in His direction. Peter tells us, "And though you have not seen Him, you love Him, and though you do not see Him now but believe in Him, you greatly rejoice with joy inexpressible and full of glory" (1 Peter 1:8).

In 2 Corinthians 3 and 4 the apostle Paul takes us one step further. Beyond the "inexpressible joy" we receive as we focus on our Lord, we are actually being changed by that very gaze!

> But we all, with unveiled face beholding as in a mirror the glory of the Lord, are being transformed into the same image from glory to glory, just as from the Lord, the Spirit.
>
> For God, who said, "Light shall shine out of darkness," is the One who has shone in our hearts to give the light of the knowledge of the glory of God in the face of Christ.

Then he adds:

> But we have this treasure in earthen vessels. (2 Corinthians 3:18 and 4:6-7)

The face of the Lord Jesus Christ is toward me. As I lift my face to Him, seeing Him through the eyes of faith, I am being changed to resemble Him. This is treasure—"the light of the glory of God in the face of Jesus Christ"—treasure which will keep increasing through all my days, no matter what life delivers to my door. This is treasure that no outside force or circumstance can ever take away from me.

"Look My way, David," the Lord is saying. "Let the eyes of your heart rest upon Me, and you will not only find Me looking back, but you will also find yourself being changed to increasingly resemble My Son!"

John tells us that as we walk with Him, we will always be in the light (1 John 1:5-7). Always in the light. We're children of the light!

Yet as I stood by the seashore that night so many years ago, I could have chosen to stand with my back to the sea. I could have said, "But God, it's so dark!" And all the while missing the glory. God would say to me, "Turn around! I'm looking toward you; why aren't you looking toward Me?"

Turn around! That's exactly what repentance is. It's changing the direction of your mind—your focus. It's realigning your thoughts to look His way. How often have we found ourselves overwhelmed by the darkness of our circumstances when all the glory of God is shining on our backs!

Drink in His forgiveness. Affirm His love before all the principalities and powers of the universe. Rest in His presence. Fill your heart with His loving gaze. God's face is *your way*—and always will be.

Chapter 6

All Knowing . . . All Wise

There are no secrets. No secret thoughts. No secret plans. No secret longings. No secret fears.

Every thought that flashes through your mind—every single one—God knows.

O LORD, You have searched me and known me.
You know my sitting down and my rising up;
You understand my thought afar off.
You comprehend my path and my lying down,
And are acquainted with all my ways.
For there is not a word on my tongue,
But behold, O LORD, You know it altogether.
You have hedged me behind and before,
And laid Your hand upon me.
Such knowledge is too wonderful for me . . .
                                    (Psalm 139:1-6 NKJV)

There is nothing about me that God doesn't know. The beautiful and the ugly. The kind and the cruel. The loving and the lustful. He knows it all.

A disturbing thought? It would seem so. Yet to David that knowledge was precious—"too wonderful." In fact, he valued God's all-knowingness so much that he closed his psalm by inviting God to search the deepest corners of his heart, to know everything to be known—even his anxious thoughts.

Do we really want anyone to know us that well? How would you feel if suddenly some Sunday morning in church all your thoughts were projected on a screen for all to read? If there were only one person there to read them besides yourself, that would be one too many. For fear of the consequences, most of us have become experts in allowing others to come only so close—to know only so much.

"Hello! How are you?"

"Great! And how are you?"

("Great?" No, I'm not great. Right now I feel like a flop, a social misfit. Why did I have to bump into him anyway? I should have stayed in bed. I wish I could be honest, but I can't. Anyway, "How are you?" is not a request for a medical history! So I'll bluff it. He wouldn't understand. Why should he understand?)

How guarded we are in sharing our most private thoughts with anyone—even those closest to us. What then is it about our all-knowing God that will make us feel as safe as David felt?

It is this. David was aware that His God was more than all-knowing—He was also all-wise. It wasn't simply God *knowing* his thoughts that impressed David, but God *understanding* them. That makes all the difference! Knowledge has to do with information; wisdom has to do with how someone uses what he knows.

I might be willing to share my thoughts with someone else if only I could be sure he or she would understand. If only this individual could see each thought in light of all that brought it about. If only he or she could see *all* my thoughts and know how they all fit together. Even those sinful thoughts—though they would still be sinful—at least it might bring some understanding as to why they were there. Yes, if I had someone like that, I wouldn't be so afraid. In fact if I knew such a person also loved me, I would find myself longing to seek his or her counsel. Of course there is no one like that . . . except God!

That is why David said, "Such knowledge is too wonderful for me." That is why he closes the psalm with the words,

Search me, O God, and know my heart;
Try me and know my anxious thoughts;
And see if there be any hurtful way in me,
And lead me in the everlasting way.

(Psalm 139:23-24)

Someone to Show Me the Way

Think of it! We have a God with whom we can be totally honest—utterly transparent—not only because He knows everything already, but also because He truly understands. No need to put on a false front before Him—trying to say the right words when we pray. Appearing pious when we are actually struggling with doubts. No matter how we feel we can tell Him. Even if we are right in the middle of sinning, He is still there. He is fully understanding (grieving, but not condemning), eager to forgive and to heal.

But doesn't sin break our fellowship with God? (How many times have you heard that?) Yes it does—but *only* if you have chosen to turn your back on Him. And if you do that, He has not rejected you; you have rejected Him.

Imagine yourself, for example, dominated by the sin of coveting—desiring something God does not want you to have. You know these desires are wrong. You sincerely wish you could stop feeling the way you do. Yes, you've confessed it. But that doesn't make it go away, does it? Confession rarely solves that problem. Anyway, how can you stop wanting something you want? Obviously, it takes more than confession to gain deliverance.

What you need is *more* than forgiveness. You need someone who understands you and your situation well enough to point the way out. Wouldn't it be tragic if at the very time you needed God the most you couldn't reach Him? But He *is* there. Ready to talk to—to listen. Someone who knows you far better than you know yourself.

God's knowing us better than we know ourselves has huge implications. Through the new covenant miracle of the new birth, God knows that we are *right now* "qualified . . . to share in the inheritance of the saints in light" (Colossians 1:12.) He knows that we are His new creations, partakers of His divine nature to such a degree that if we died right now, we would belong in His holy heaven.

But so often the collection of rubbish in the computer mechanism of our brains, the pressures of the world, and Satan's deception begin to loom so large that they cloud our awareness of reality. We begin to function in fantasy—the fantasy that we really *are* of this world when we aren't. The fantasy that sin is our friend rather than our enemy. Time and again I have found myself right there—so deceived, so defeated.

But there is no space for fantasy before the throne of grace! Knowing us far better than we know ourselves, He affirms our royal lineage, our union with His Son. Though we forget, He never does. As a fresh breeze sweeps away stale air, so our God breathes into us the reality of our citizenship, reminding us that the kingdom in which we fit best is characterized by "righteousness and peace and joy in the Holy Spirit."

Is "omniscience," then, a cold theological idea? Far from it! Because of who God is—all-knowing and all-wise—He will never "take something the wrong way." He will never misunderstand. No "hidden skeleton" that might fall out of some forgotten closet would ever cause Him to say, "Well now, I didn't know *that* about you." No. Not now. Not forever!

Knowledge by Experience

One thousand years after David's time our God added something to Himself—a most wonderful "something"—that He did not have before. How could that have been possible? He has always known everything about us. But He decided to "know" us in a new way, even more deeply than before. He accomplished this by becoming one of us. By becoming a man. Because of this strangest of miracles, His knowledge about us now is *by experience*.

> Since then we have a great high priest who has passed through the heavens, Jesus the Son of God, let us hold fast our confession. For we do not have a high priest who cannot sympathize with our weaknesses, but one who has been tempted in all things as we are, yet without sin. Let us therefore draw near with confidence to the throne of grace, that we may receive mercy and may find grace to help in time of need. (Hebrews 4:14-16)

Jesus, my great High Priest, has actually felt every pressure, every temptation, every weakness I will ever know. What a huge price He paid even *before* He went to the cross. How strange it must have been for Him to suffer through all those years of human frailty. And why? So that when you and I approach His throne we will never tell him something that will be foreign to Him. No, He never sinned. But that very fact means that the pressures of temptation He endured went *beyond* the points where we so often break down.

This truth struck home to me in the bluntest of ways when God called my father home to be with Him. I loved him very much. Before that time when I spoke at funerals and met with bereaved families, I sincerely tried to sympathize with them. There were a few times I found myself weeping with them. But after I lost my dad, every funeral since has been different. Now I *know*, I know *in experience* just how they feel.

Consider how far God willingly went in order to "know" us.

Perfect Ends, Perfect Means

Someone has defined perfect wisdom as the ability to choose perfect ends (or goals) and to arrive at those ends by perfect means. You and I can easily dream up *perfect ends*, but the *perfect means*—that's something else.

We usually have little trouble trusting God about the "ends." His kingdom *will* come. We know that. But often we find it hard to trust God as to the means of getting us to those ends. Perhaps it is because we have so much trouble with them ourselves.

Am I the only person who can take a perfectly good day and cover it over with gloom simply by watching a half hour of the evening news? What will be the next explosive crisis in the world? What's the economy going to do? What new atrocity will sicken us all? Before I know it, I have laid on myself the worries of the whole world. It's one thing to have genuine concern for hurting people, but it's quite another thing to make their worries my own.

In trying to get our bearings once again, especially in those times when the hurts touch us more personally, there is one verse we often turn to. Many of us know it by heart.

And we know that God causes all things to work together for good to those who love God, to those who are called according to His purpose. (Romans 8:28)

What marvelous words! They are just as good as they sound. Note that the verse begins with the word "and." Important? Yes, because it shows that verse 28 is part of a flow of thought—a flow that makes this verse even more significant. In the preceding verses Paul reminds us that Christians are to expect suffering not only because we are to share in Christ's sufferings, but also because we still belong to a groaning, fragile creation. Yet no matter how deep the groaning, we are to take heart because God has chosen to do something very special for us during those hurting times.

All of us have been in circumstances where the weight of concern or uncertainty presses with such intensity that, though we know we should pray, we simply do not know what to say. There are times when I have found myself repeatedly saying "O Father, O Father, O Father . . . !" without saying much of anything else. I would try to think of something else, but all other words seemed out of place. I did not know what to ask—I didn't know what to say.

In those darkest of times our most marvelous, all-wise God does our praying for us!

> For we do not know how to pray as we should, but the Spirit Himself intercedes for us with groanings too deep for words; and He who searches the hearts knows what the mind of the Spirit is, because He intercedes for the saints *according to the will of God.* (8:26-27)

Immediately following these words we find Romans 8:28! All of the "means" toward God's perfect "ends" are perfect too. Why? Because a perfect prayer authored by an all-wise God will most certainly have a perfect answer—He intercedes for us "according to the will of God." Now that's encouragement! Yet there is more.

This same flow of thought is climaxed by Paul reminding us that if God willingly "did not spare His own Son, but delivered Him up for us all, how will He not also with Him freely give us *all things*?" (verse 32). Could anything more be added to that?

Yes! This One who gives out of His limitless wisdom and purpose assures us that nothing "shall be able to separate us from His love."

Perfect means and perfect ends are all in His sovereign control!

A Tale of Two Trusting Families

Many of our "whys" will have to wait until heaven for answers. Yet there are times when God allows us *now* to look back on one of those dark memories from the past and see it from the vantage point of His perfect wisdom. How could something so wrong, so tragic, ever "work together for good"? And yet it did! It makes sense now, even as Joseph discovered when at last he embraced his brothers. (Remember the story in Genesis 37-50?) If in those moments we are privileged to taste a bit of the wonder of God's wisdom, what will heaven be like when at last "I shall know fully, just as I also have been fully known"?

To see this more clearly, let's create a situation.

Imagine with me two farmers: One raises wheat, and the other, down the road a ways, raises tomatoes. Both farmers have balloon payments coming due on their mortgages. Everything hinges on harvest time. A crop failure would mean the loss of the farm. Let's complicate things a bit more. In each family the farmer's wife is very sick and in need of expensive surgery. Without it, there is little hope of improvement. And one more thing: Both families are faithfully walking with God.

It's evening. Each family listens intently to the weather forecast. There's a fifty-fifty chance of rain this particular night. The wheat farmer is well aware that his fields need one more heavy, soaking rain to bring the grain through to harvest. With that, the farm could be theirs and his wife might be able to walk again.

Down the road, the other farmer knows that his tomatoes are right at their prime—ready to be harvested. But if the rains come, not only will his fields become a muddy bog, making it impossible to harvest, but also the moisture could trigger a blight that would destroy the entire crop. Without the harvest, they will lose everything.

After the weather report, each family gathers around the bed in the room where Mom is resting. Each family prays—Mom and Dad and a couple of children.

One by one they lift their hearts to God. "Dear Lord," prays the wheat family, "You know what is at stake. Please, Lord, send the rain. You know how much we want to please You. If only You would bring the rain, Lord, it would mean so much to us. And we would give You all the praise. In Jesus' name, Amen."

Down the road, four equally earnest prayers ascend to God. "O Father, please, please keep the rain from falling. Everything depends on this harvest. Thank You for listening. We trust You, in Jesus' name, Amen." As the younger child slides off the bed she turns to her mother and says, "Don't worry, Mommie. I know He will answer our prayers. Goodnight!"

It's silent now, except for the wind whistling around the corners of the farmhouses. The hours pass by. What will happen? Here's where we play God. We could arrange to have the rain follow the fence line between the two farms—wet on one side and dry on the other. But that's not the way things usually are. What will we do? Let's find out.

Suddenly the wheat farmer wakens: He heard a tinkle on the sheet-metal roof of the garage. He holds his breath. Just one drop? Is that all? No! In moments the tinkles multiply until they sound like thunder on the roof. Two children come running down the hall—they've heard it too. Bouncing on Mommie's bed they shout, "God heard our prayers! He heard them! Isn't it exciting?" Once again the family gathers with tears of joy, praising the Lord.

But down the road the other farmer also hears the first raindrop. Sitting up in bed, he too holds his breath. "Perhaps it will stop! Please, Father. Oh please!" But no. Louder and louder the sheets of rain sweep over his home, splattering against the windows. He sees in his mind those fields so full of lush tomatoes, beaten down, drowning in the mud. Quietly, he slips back beneath the blankets. There's no sound of children's feet running down the hall in this home. But in the darkness he feels the gentle squeeze of his wife's hand on his shoulder as she whispers, "Sweetheart, it's all right. God cares. He knows."

Next morning—breakfast time with the wheat family. And what a breakfast it is! Mom scurries around the kitchen in her wheelchair. Everybody is so excited. "Daddy!" one of the children says, "everything is all right, isn't it? We can pay off the farm and Mommie will be well again! Isn't God wonderful?"

And the tomato farm: There's breakfast there too—but it's very quiet. Father says he'll ask the blessing. But instead, there's a long, long pause. Finally, unable to hold back the tears, he speaks between his sobs. "Lord . . . we prayed. We really thought we prayed the way we should . . . And Lord, we don't understand. It . . . seemed so right that You would answer. But thank You, Lord. You do love us . . . we know that, and we'll keep right on trusting You no matter what happens now." The silence that follows is broken by some very hurting "whys," and Daddy finds he has no answers.

Since this is our story, let's not stop it now. Let's imagine five years have gone by. We are walking again down the lane by those same two farms. The first thing that catches our eye is the freshly painted barn and a new car parked in front of one farmhouse. Out behind, stretching as far as we can see are rolling hills covered with wheat. Let's move up close by the window.

There's Mom, standing,—looking robust and strong—walking around the kitchen and fixing breakfast. The kids are just coming in—five years older now. And there's Dad, taking off his boots after the early morning chores. "Family," he says, "do you know what day this is? This is the fifth anniversary of the greatest crisis our family has ever gone through. Do you remember that night we prayed? God heard our prayer, didn't He?"

"Dad, wasn't it great? Mom's well now. The farm is all ours, isn't it, Dad?"

"That's right. In fact, God has blessed us more than I had ever dreamed. He deserves not only our thanks, but our lives! So let's gather around the table and each one of us tell Him how much we love Him."

What might we find if we stopped in at the house down the road? There it is. Such a contrast! It looks so rundown. And the name on the front of the barn—it's been changed. The family's still there, but they're tenants now. Let's step up closer to the kitchen window. There are the kids coming in along with Dad, fresh from his morning chores. Dad walks down the hall, and a few moments later returns, pushing his wife's wheelchair close to the kitchen table.

Before asking the blessing, Dad turns to his family and says, "Family, do you know what day this is? This is the anniversary of the greatest crisis our family has ever gone through. Do you remember what happened five years ago?"

As they recall that devastating night, the family joins hands. Dad prays, "O God, thank You! Thank You for Your grace and goodness. At first that night seemed like such a catastrophe, and yet . . . O Father, how You have taught us things about Yourself! You've opened the door to a knowledge of You through our suffering we never would have known any other way. God, You're so good!"

Do things such as these in our made-up story actually happen? Yes they do! Stories like this one could be told thousands of times over by Christian steelworkers, shut-ins, students, missionaries, teachers, shopkeepers. Unique stories . . . stories only they know about. Yet woven through them all are the threads that lead back to one all-knowing, all-wise, most high God. Oh, the wonder of the mysteries of our God!

Amen, blessing and glory and *wisdom* and thanksgiving and honor and power and might, be to our God forever and ever. Amen. (Revelation 7:12)

Chapter 7

Holiness Is Happiness

What's the first idea that comes to your mind when you hear the word *holy?*

Hushed reverence? Absolute, unbending, somber piety?

Words like that remind me of a great-aunt I had. Aunt Ida. Once in a long while when I was quite young our family would pay her a visit. Before entering her very proper, everything-in-its-place Pasadena apartment, we children dutifully received the standard parental lecture.

"Be quiet.
Don't touch anything.
Sit still until we leave."

And we did. We all knew Aunt Ida loved us. Each of us received her ample embrace when we first arrived. I can still feel those hard corset stays when my turn came to suffer momentary claustrophobia.

I don't remember what my brother and my sisters received, but every Christmas without fail my Aunt Ida sent me the same present. Candied grapefruit peels. They were awful. But it was worse when I had to sit down to write her afterward. I felt like choking as I wrote, "Dear Aunt Ida, thank you for the . . . ."

Yes, "hushed reverence, somber piety." That was my Aunt Ida. It wasn't that she didn't love me. It was just that she wasn't any fun.

Is holiness like that?

Is God like that?

What Isaiah Saw

Most of my life I've thought of the word *holy* as being a cold word. Absolute. Unbending. Remote. Like staring up for a long time into a dark, yet sparkling night sky with its myriad stars hung in a vastness of empty space. Pure light. Cold light. Impossibly distant. Utterly unmoved by life way down here.

That's the way it seems to come across as we read the description of God's holiness in Isaiah 6. Whatever Isaiah saw and heard was so awesome that it marked the rest of his life. After that encounter, his special title for God became "The Holy One of Israel."

Let's listen to him for a moment—and perhaps get a peek over his shoulder.

> In the year of King Uzziah's death, I saw the LORD sitting on a throne, lofty and exalted, with the train of His robe filling the temple. Seraphim stood above Him, each having six wings; with two he covered his face, and with two he covered his feet, and with two he flew. And one called out to another and said,
>
> "Holy, Holy, Holy, is the LORD of hosts,
> The whole earth is full of His glory."
>
> And the foundations of the thresholds trembled at the voice of him who called out, while the temple was filling with smoke. Then I said,
>
> "Woe is me, for I am ruined!
> Because I am a man of unclean lips,
> And I live among a people of unclean lips;
> For my eyes have seen the King, the LORD of hosts."
>
> (Isaiah 6:1-5)

The Hebrew word for "holy" expresses the thought of something being *separated*. So in Isaiah's mind, the seraphim were actually crying out, "Separated, Separated, Separated, is the LORD of hosts."

God—separated? How?

From what Isaiah tells us, it would appear that we are to think of God being separated—holy—in at least three ways.

LOFTY AND EXALTED. First, Isaiah was impressed with God

being "way up there"—lofty and exalted. Separated in the sense of His being high above His creation. This is closely parallel with something God would tell him years later:

> For thus says the High and Lofty One who inhabits eternity, whose name is Holy; "I dwell in the high and holy place." (Isaiah 57:15 NKJV)

David and Daniel knew God this way, too. Often they spoke of Him as "the Most High God." You and I must never forget that. Our God is of such majesty that to think rightly of Him we must confess His loftiness and bow low before Him, Him whose throne transcends the universe.

A favorite assignment I've given my Bible college students for many years has been to require that some time during the course they spend a minimum of fifteen minutes, lying on their backs, looking up at the stars contemplating the lofty holiness of God. My hope has been that this would begin a lifetime habit. (The only hitch in the assignment was that they were not to do it in pairs!)

GLORY AND SPLENDOR. But Isaiah also understood God's separatedness to involve the vast difference between His transcendent glory and the relative drabness of our fallen humanity. The train of His robe filled the temple, Isaiah remembered, and seraph called out to seraph, "The whole earth is full of His glory."

GLORY is one of those mysterious biblical words that point toward the splendor of God. Paul tells us God "dwells in unapproachable light." We can then assume that if we possessed seraphim's eyes we would be able to see the entire earth covered with the radiant majesty of God. It is there because God is there. Someday "The earth will be filled with the *knowledge* of the glory of the LORD" (Habakkuk 2:14). But not yet.

BURNING PURITY. Loftiness . . . glory . . . but most of all, the separateness of God's purity—His absolute moral perfection. Isaiah's anguished response to the seraphim song of God's holiness was this:

> Woe is me, for I am ruined!
> Because I am a man of unclean lips,
> And I live among a people of unclean lips;
> For my eyes have seen the King, the LORD of hosts.

74 Holiness Is Happiness

Can you imagine Isaiah's sheer terror? No place to hide! No alternative but death itself. He knew his impurity could not coexist in the presence of God's spotlessness.

Holiness Incarnate

Though in some mysterious way God cleansed Isaiah that day so he could become His prophet, the world had yet to wait seven hundred years for Jesus, God's perfect answer to man's unholiness. (How glibly we speak of those long stretches of history between Bible stories! *Seven hundred years.* Dark, hurting, waiting, longing years.)

Then it happpened.

> The angel said to her, "Do not be afraid, Mary; for you have found favor with God. And behold, you will conceive in your womb, and bear a son, and you shall name Him Jesus." (Luke 1:30-31)

> "How will this be," Mary asked the angel, "since I am a virgin?" The angel answered, "The *Holy* Spirit will come upon you, and the power of the *Most High* will overshadow you. So the *holy* one to be born will be called the Son of God." (1:34-35 NIV)

And indeed He was. Thirty plus years of unblemished purity—childhood, youth, and young adulthood.

At the end of His trial, Pilate could say, "I find no fault in Him."

Nailed next to Jesus on another cross, a dying felon gasped, "We are receiving what we deserve for our deeds, but this man has done nothing wrong."

And years later Peter would write:

> Knowing that you were not redeemed with perishable things like silver or gold . . . but with precious blood, as of a lamb unblemished and spotless, the blood of Christ. (1 Peter 1:18-19)

Through the scourging, to the cross, into the eternal wrath of God this Jesus went. "Pierced for our transgressions . . . crushed for our iniquities." This One who "knew no sin became sin on our behalf."

Then all the way back—risen and ascended, up to The Glory from whence He had come. Back where hosts of heaven were still singing,

Holy, holy, holy is the Lord God, the Almighty, who was, and who is, and who is to come. (Revelation 4:8)

The writer to the Hebrews adds his own "Amen" when he writes:

For it was fitting that we should have such a high priest, holy, inno-cent, undefiled, separated from sinners and exalted above the heavens. (7:26)

"Separated from sinners"? That sounds discouraging. How can we dare to come close? Should we too cry out "Woe is me!"? Because of Jesus, God's amazing answer to you and me is "Come up close . . . come very close."

"Hurry" Joins the Family

Many years ago when my wife and I were first married, we looked with surprise out of the kitchen window one day at a blur of black and white as it zipped around the corner of our home. In the days that followed we discovered that the "blur" was actually a terribly frightened stray dog. In time she would dare to drink our water and eat our food—but never when we were around. The moment she caught a glance of us at the door she would run away as though she knew she didn't belong. Certainly she was in no way worthy of us. How could she trust our invitations to come closer?

Gradually her fears subsided, and instead of running she would simply sit a ways off and cock her little head. She so much wanted to belong—to be close. But could she, would she, trust our gentle words? No, they were too good to be true. To think that anyone would consider her to be of value—that someone would truly desire her!

Finally, one day her rigid pose and cocked head changed in an instant into that familiar black and white blur of speed we had so often seen before. But this time it ended in one huge leap right into our arms. She belonged! She was safe.

In the months that followed, little "Hurry" entered into all the rights and privileges befitting a member of our family. Closeness would be hers the rest of her life. She had taken us at our word.

Can we take God at His Word—incredible as it seems? Can we

believe Him and respond to Him as He offers invitation after invitation through His Word?

> Let us therefore draw near with confidence to the throne of grace, that we may receive mercy and may find grace to help in time of need. (Hebrews 4:16)

> We have confidence to enter the holy place by the blood of Jesus . . . let us draw near with a sincere heart in full assurance of faith, having our hearts sprinkled clean from an evil conscience. (Hebrews 10:19-22)

When we pray, we too come to where The Glory is. Do we truly belong there? God's answer is "Yes! Forever!" Because of Jesus.

Holiness Is Happiness

One of my favorite areas of teaching is the Old Testament prophets. It has been my special delight to awaken my students to a section of the Bible most Christians avoid. Personally, I will never praise God enough for the radical effect this part of Scripture has had in my life. One revolutionary effect was the way it changed my understanding of holiness.

A passage in Isaiah forms the climax for the entire first half of the book. In poetic form it depicts what life will be like on the far side of God's judgment of the world.

Listen . . .

> The wilderness and the desert will be glad,
> And the desert will rejoice and blossom;
> Like the crocus
> It will blossom profusely
> And rejoice with rejoicing and shout of joy. . . .
> Then the lame will leap like a deer,
> And the tongue of the dumb will shout for joy. . . .
> And the ransomed of the LORD will return,
> And come with joyful shouting to Zion,
> With everlasting joy upon their heads.
> They will find gladness and joy,
> And sorrow and sighing will flee away. (35:1-10)

That's beautiful, but what does it have to do with holiness? Everything! Because Isaiah tells us where all this pure pleasure will take place. Where?

And a highway will be there, a roadway,
And it will be called "the Highway *of Holiness.*" (35:8)

On this highway to the city of God people will "shout for joy," and "leap like a deer." There will be "everlasting joy." Sorrow and sighing will not simply be gone; they will "flee away." Along this highway even the blossoming crocus "will rejoice with rejoicing and shout of joy."

What is on this highway of holiness? All the happiness our hearts long for. Whatever our "cold" concept of God's holiness was before, whatever false "Aunt Ida" images we've carried around for years, they must give way to the truth: Holiness *is* happiness!

You will show me the path of life;
In Your presence is fullness of joy;
At Your right hand are pleasures forevermore.
(Psalm 16:11 NKJV)

Mystery of mysteries . . . somehow to bow trembling before God's lofty, holy throne will be perfectly compatible with leaping and shouting for joy—"pleasures forevermore." How do these thoughts fit into your picture of holiness? For me, they were revolutionary!

Are these ideas found only in isolated passages in the Bible? Not at all. Listen, for example, to these expressions from Psalms 46-48.

There is a river whose streams make glad the city of God, The *holy* dwelling places of the Most High. (46:4)

O clap your hands, all peoples;
Shout to God with the voice of joy
For the LORD Most High is to be feared,
A great King over all the earth . . . .
God sits on his *holy* throne. (47:1-2 and 47:8)

Great is the LORD, and greatly to be praised
in the city of our God,
    in the mountain of *his holiness.*
Beautiful for situation, the joy of the whole earth,
is Mount Zion . . . (48:1-2 KJV).

Happiness . . . Then and Now

Yes, happiness is holiness. Yet someone may be saying, "Well, that will be true someday, but not now. For now, God's call to holiness

is a call to sacrifice. Saying 'No' to our desires in order to follow
that hard, self-rejecting road of discipleship. Oh sure, there's joy in
knowing we are pleasing God. But certainly there is no joy in saying
'No' to sin in order to say 'Yes' to what is holy. To do that is to go
against everything we are. And that's tough."

Somewhere along the way in our effort to underline the insidious-
ness of sin, we have lost sight of the bigness of the miracle God
performed when we were born again. And that's a tragedy. It seems
so easy for us to affirm any Scripture passage which underlines the
problems Christians will have with sin. But we find it hard to take
at face value those passages that tell us the Christian's nature is to
produce holiness.

Jesus said, "Blessed are the pure in heart for they shall see God."
Will you see God someday? Do you believe that if you died right
this instant you would go to be with God—dwelling happily in His
holiness? I hope your answer is an enthusiastic "Yes!" Well then,
when did you receive that "pure heart"? Does God have some sort
of "spiritual carwash" somewhere in between your death and your
arrival in heaven? Listen to what God says:

> Therefore if any man is in Christ, he is a new creature; the old things
> passed away; behold, new things have come. (2 Corinthians 5:17)

> How shall we who died to sin still live in it? . . . Even so consider
> yourself dead to sin, but alive to God in Christ Jesus. (Romans 6:2
> and 6:11)

God has made a marvelous transformation in the deepest level of
your personhood. In your "inner man" *you* delight in God's "law"
(Romans 7:22). Tragically, so many Christians continue to think of
themselves "according to the flesh." Apparently they believe that
"the principle at work in [their] members" represents who they most
deeply are—even though Romans 7:16-25 says the exact opposite!
Yes, those "members" do belong to you. And you are responsible.
But keep in mind, they haven't been redeemed yet. Don't expect
this body and brain of yours to neatly fall in line with holiness.

But you, *you*, have been born again. For you, holiness is happiness.
Personal purity is your "cup of tea." Your flesh has been deceiving
you long enough! The spotless purity of God's "highway of holiness"
was made for you. Now! (See 1 John 3:6-10.)

May you increasingly believe God concerning what He says about you. And as you do, to your surprise, you will discover that saying "No" to sin *is* saying "Yes" to life, to joy, to everything your heart most deeply desires. Sin is your enemy, not your friend. For God— and you—holiness *is* happiness.

And as the bridegroom rejoices over the bride,
So your God will rejoice over you.

(Isaiah 62:5)

He will exult over you with joy,
He will be quiet in His love,
He will rejoice over you with shouts of joy.

(Zephaniah 3:17)

Chapter 8

The Way that He Loves

There are so many facets to the character of God.

You and I could dig deeply into the mysteries of His infinite wisdom, His limitless power, His unwavering justice. We could contemplate the fact that He never changes, never ages, never tires, never fails.

We could accept all these truths—and ten thousand more—yet still feel an emptiness within. A hurting question still aching for an answer.

Does He love me?

What is it to me that He is absolutely pure and powerful—if He doesn't care about me?

Looking ahead to a time when his countrymen would be captives in Babylon, Isaiah wrote about the greatness of God. There would be deep discouragement and doubt among the exiles. They would begin to wonder whether God even knew they were there—much less cared two cents about what would happen to them.

In response, Isaiah tells them—and us—that God

. . has measured the waters in the hollow of his hand,
And marked off the heavens by the span.

(Isaiah 40:12)

This God measures the distances between stars with His thumb and little finger! He has

> . . . calculated the dust of the earth by the measure,
> And weighed the mountains in a balance,
> And the hills in a pair of scales. (40:12)

His wisdom soars above our comprehension, for

> Who has directed the Spirit of the LORD,
> Or as His counselor has informed Him?
> With whom did He consult and who gave Him understanding?
> And who taught Him in the path of justice and taught Him knowledge,
> And informed Him of the way of understanding? (40:13-14)

If you wanted to present an offering to God, you could burn all of the mighty cedars of Lebanon and offer up all of its animals for sacrifice—their smoke billowing toward heaven like a massive volcano (40:16). And that would not be enough.

He is not impressed by great armies, vast nuclear arsenals, or space-piercing lasers, for

> . . . the nations are like a drop from a bucket,
> And are regarded as a speck of dust on the scales; . . .
> All the nations are as nothing before Him,
> They are regarded by Him as less than nothing and
>   meaningless. (40:15-17)

Kings, presidents, prime ministers, and dictators hold no sway with Him. He heeds neither parliament nor congress nor assembly. As a matter of fact,

> He it is who reduces rulers to nothing,
> Who makes the judges of the earth meaningless.
> Scarcely have they been planted,
> Scarcely have they been sown,
> Scarcely has their stock taken root in the earth,
> But He merely blows on them, and they wither,
> And the storm carries them away like stubble. (40:23-24)

How great is this God? Don't sit on your couch and wonder. Don't lie on your bed and stare at the ceiling. Don't pore over heavy theological books in a library. Get out of your house in the dark of night, get away from the city lights, and

Lift up your eyes on high
And see who has created these stars,
The One who leads forth their host by number,
He calls them all by name;
Because of the greatness of His might and the strength of His power
Not one of them is missing. (40:26)

He calls them all by name! A trillion trillion suns in the infinite depths . . . and even the farthest star, the last flaming outpost at the frayed black edges of God's universe bears a name.

"Do you not know?" the prophet cries out. "Have you not heard?"

The everlasting God, the LORD, the Creator of the ends of the earth
Does not become weary or tired.
His understanding is inscrutable. (40:28)

Yes, He is great. Yes, He is wise and just and mighty beyond words. I can believe all that.

But does He *love* me?

And if He doesn't . . . ?

Anticipating that question, the Holy Spirit moved Isaiah to pen these words before all the others . . .

Like a shepherd He will tend His flock,
In His arms He will gather the lambs,
And carry them in His bosom;
He will gently lead the nursing ewes. (40:11)

This awesome God would take me up in His arms as though I were a newborn lamb. He leads me gently as He would a nursing ewe burdened with the care of her young.

He *does* love me. He *does* care.

Then is that what love is—caring for someone? Yes, certainly, but it's only a beginning.

There is a story that came out of China many years ago of a missionary who found it necessary to be gone from his family for an extended time. Aware that his leaving would not be understood by his youngest daughter, he placed in his coat pocket a rare treat in that part of China—a bright red apple—to give her as he boarded the train.

Finally the moment came. He embraced his wife and then each of the older children. And then it was his little girl's turn. Picking her up in his arms, he pressed the apple into her chubby hand, hoping that this special gift would soften the impact of his leaving. But instead, as he looked back from the slowly departing train, he saw the apple slip from her hand and roll across the platform. Tears streaming down her face, she ran alongside the train sobbing, "Daddy, I don't want what you give—I want *you!*"

That's it! That is the wonder of God's love! He does not simply give "things." He gives Himself.

But how far did God go in giving Himself?

"We Know Love by This . . ."

Think back with me to that magical moment in your childhood when you first discovered the power of a magnifying glass. It was a warm summer day, wasn't it? You borrowed the glass from the desk drawer and took it outside in the sunshine. Then you held it at just the right distance to form a tiny circle of brilliant light in a small pile of dry grass or leaves. (Maybe you were just mean enough to aim that spot at the opening of an ant hill.)

In a few moments it began to smoke—then burst into flame. Somehow that glass lens was able to gather the heat from all the rays of sunlight striking its surface, and direct this combined, sizzling intensity to that one spot.

Now picture the world—a globe covered with billions of people. And above it, like rays from the sun, the blinding intensity of the righteous judgment and wrath of God bearing down upon the human race. Then imagine a great cosmic magnifying glass—as wide as the world—placed in between, gathering all of that intensity of burning wrath and focusing it on one spot. On one individual. On Jesus, nailed to the cross.

For you see, Jesus did not simply give Himself to die as anyone else might die. Far, far more than that! In His dying He gave Himself to be a receptacle—a container. First, to be filled up with our sin, and then, to be filled with the white-hot wrath of an infinitely holy God. Wrath that should have fallen on the entire human race—on me. Yet all of it was focused on Him! Can we imagine its intensity?

Can we begin to read between the lines as He cried out, "My God, My God, why have You forsaken Me?"

He who became our sin, became the object of the wrath we deserved.

We know love by this, that He laid down His life for us. (1 John 3:16)

His Choice . . . and Ours

Love. *Agape* love. "An act of the will whereby God gives Himself to us for our good." Another cold definition? No! Far from it. More than a warm feeling. More than simply caring. God gave Himself for us—to us.

Agape is one of several Greek words translated into just one English word, "love." It is by far the most common "love" word in the New Testament. It is a kind of love that has nothing to do with the quality of the ones being loved (how lovable we are), but everything to do with the quality of the Lover. It is not first a feeling, but rather a deliberate choice—an act of the will. It is God saying to you, "I commit Myself to actively give you all that I am."

He who did not spare His own Son, but delivered Him up for us all, how will He not also with Him freely give us all things? (Romans 8:32)

Since John tells us that "God is love," it is hard to imagine anything of greater importance to God than that His love would find complete fulfillment. God has already made the choice of giving Himself to us. And what He gives is of supreme worth. Yet it is at this point that we confront a most remarkable thing. You and I can frustrate the fulfillment of that love. His love must be *received*.

Unreceived love is frustrated love. It is unfulfilled—like beautiful music drifting across an empty landscape where there are no ears to hear. God has allowed us to make the terrible choice of spurning His love. He allows us to say in our pride, "I don't need God's help. I don't need anybody's help. I'll make it on my own."

"You just tell me what God expects me to do for Him and I'll do it. I'll share my talents, my time—even my money. If the church has a need, you just let me know, I'll be the first to volunteer. But this 'receiving' thing . . . that's not for me, I'm not going to be a debtor to anyone—not even to God. Listen, I've got my pride just like anybody else."

Pride. Good ol' smug American self-reliance—the greatest barrier to the gospel. The scourge of the Genesis Fall. For this reason we who are Christians need to be most careful in the way we present the gospel. The grace of God is a gift. All of it. Forgiveness, being reconciled to God, eternal life—are all gifts. The gospel is not "will you *give* your heart to God?" It isn't giving anything to God. The gospel is "will you *receive* Jesus as your Savior and Lord?" Only in that act is God's love fulfilled.

"But wait!" someone objects. "What about the story of the rich young ruler? When he asked Jesus what he had to do to obtain eternal life, the Lord told him to go and sell all he had and give it to the poor, and then follow Him. So you see? To be a Christian you have to give up a lot for God and then try your best to follow Jesus."

Let's take a second look at that story. The idea of "giving up something" wasn't really the point of that conversation at all. Here was a man who wanted eternal life. He wanted what God alone could give. Yet he was unable to open his hands and heart to receive that gift because they were already filled with images of his own riches. His dreams, his hopes, and his values were tied up in his possessions and Jesus knew it. In a sense, Jesus was saying to him, "You say you want Me . . . yet you don't have any room for Me. You can't receive God's gift—your arms are already too full of your own things. Drop them and receive! Let them go. Open yourself to Me!"

It's still that way. Nothing's changed. What must I do with a God who says "I love you"? Give Him something? Bargain with Him? No, just one thing . . . unconditionally receive His self-giving—Himself.

Just receive.

Receiving: An Object Lesson

When I was a boy, our family moved to a ranch in southern California, where we had acres of rolling hills to explore. My big dream was to get a dog. But not just any dog. I had my heart set on an English setter. I can't begin to calculate all the time I spent reading about English setters—studying their pictures down to the smallest detail. To me, there was no dog like a setter anywhere in the world.

One day my dad gave me the word I'd been waiting for. "Okay, son," he said, "you can get your setter."

Together, Dad and I went down to the kennel. I spent the better part of an hour examining a litter of fine English setter pups. I tried to be objective—to look for all the qualities the books tell you to look for in a champion setter. The right ears and eyes and bones and tail and all that. When I walked out with that little fellow in my arms, I was sure I had the pick of the litter—the most beautiful pup I had ever seen. I called him "Mike."

In the months that followed he received the best care I knew how to give. A solid redwood doghouse with a cedar-shake roof. The best food. But most of all, the best of my love. Yet as the months went by, one fact—one terrible fact—became all too clear. Mike didn't want me. He didn't want my love. After a time, he didn't even want my food. I'd put out the dish for him and call, "Here, Mike! Here, Mike!" But Mike would not come. Or if he did, he would slink around the side of the house, pedigreed tail between his legs, work his way up to the dish, wolf down his food, and then slink away again.

When the cold winter nights came I used to long for him to sit by the fire with me. I just wanted him to lie beside me near the hearth so I could scratch under his neck and give him a big hug and let him lick my face.

But he never came when I called. And winter went by.

He may have been a good watchdog; he may have chased away the rabbits from our garden—I really don't remember. I do know that eventually he discovered that if he ran full speed into the wire mesh surrounding our chicken pen, the chickens would become a squawking brown cloud piling up against the far side of the pen. And once in awhile, one of those terrified hens would just manage to clear the top of the fence—and Mike would kill it and carry it away.

We tried everything to get him to stop. Yelling at him. Beating him (with a rolled up newspaper). Providing him more than enough to eat. My dad even suggested tying a dead chicken right up close under his jaw and letting it rot there. Perhaps that might cure him. But nothing worked. Mike simply didn't care.

Finally one day—a day I knew eventually had to come—one of the hired hands followed my dog over a hill on the far side of the ranch, while I waited behind. I knew what was going to happen. And it did. I winced as a single shot echoed back through the hills. Mike was dead . . . and rightly so.

Undaunted, a few days later—it didn't take me long—I asked, "Dad, can I try again?" And Dad said yes. Off we went to the kennel to look at a whole new litter of setter puppies. But this time I didn't look for the finest pup. Instead, I waited for one of them to come running to me. And one did. I picked him up—a little ball of silky speckled black and white fur, his heart racing like a motor—and he slobbered all over my face. I took him home with me and named him Mike. (I was stubborn.)

Maybe you can guess the rest of the story. Mike became everything I had ever dreamed of in a dog. He wanted my love. He lived for my love. I wanted Mike, and Mike wanted me.

On winter nights, Mike waited eagerly to be invited in. Pressing against the big chair in front of the fireplace, as close to me as he could be, Mike relished every touch of love. In the spring, out on the hills with the tractor, Mike would run circles around me all day long. And every time I'd stop and climb down, Mike would be there to receive a big hug or to rest his big head on my knee. When water came running down the irrigation furrows, Mike would stretch out smack dab in the middle of a furrow close to where I stood. And then get up and shake that muddy water all over me. Of course he meant it to cool me off!

When I went away to college a couple of hundred miles away, I would try to get home whenever I could. It would usually be late at night when I started up that long, curving road to the ranch house on top of the hill. Mom and Dad would be sound asleep, but Mike heard the sound of my car long before I came around the last bend. Coming to a stop, I could see him dancing in the head- lights. A moment later, Mike would crash into the driver's seat and let me hug him and love him to my heart's content.

Years later, sitting on the edge of my bunk in a small, stark seminary dorm room down in Dallas, Texas, I opened a letter from Mom. "We did everything we could do," she wrote, "but Mike had got fox fever. The veterinarian tried too, but he told us there wasn't any cure. We loved him as you would have done. We made him as comfortable as we could. But yesterday, Mike died." I remember falling back on my bunk in that lonely dorm room and crying and crying until the ink was all smeared.

Mike had let me love him.

He had received my self-giving with pleasure. His greatest delight was to be close to me. I had lost a friend who never wearied of receiving my love.

What can we say then about our infinitely self-giving God? Some of us have developed such unbalanced concepts of God. The awesome supreme Judge of the universe before whom all heaven trembles? Yes, He is all of that. But first . . . He is love. He is the God who longs to fill our lives and our days with the wealth of His presence. A God who cherishes our companionship.

How do I, as a born-again child of God, respond to my Father's self-giving? By offering myself as a gift to Him.

> With eyes wide open to the mercies of God, I beg you, my brothers, as an act of intelligent worship, to give him your bodies, as a living sacrifice. (Romans 12:1, Phillips)

It's like lifting an empty cup—a cup that God continues to fill with Himself. From the overflow, I give myself to others. And in so doing, "the love of God has truly been perfected" (1 John 2:5).

Loved by the Inventor

Yet there are times when we find ourselves unable to receive His love . . . times when our lives are so full of our own plans and schemes and drummed-up self-sufficiency that there is no room for the self-giving of God.

In these times, God often finds it necessary to bring us into the painful realization of our personal inadequacy.

Not all the things we cling to are evil in themselves. Yet they *get in the way*—they frustrate our capacity to receive the love of God.

So, firmly and lovingly, He plucks them from our grip. And that is so painful! Let's say, for example, that your feelings of self-confidence and security are wrapped up in your job. You've done good work. Climbed the ladder. Provided for your family. Achieved a level of excellence. But then something happens. The business collapses; you're fired or laid off; your health falls apart; you run into a serious relational problem. Suddenly your feelings of security scatter to the winds.

How could God allow such a thing to happen to one of His own?

Not because He doesn't love us, but because our arms are too full to receive His great love . . . because our hands cling too tightly to shreds of tinsel and worthless trinkets . . . because we have somehow forgotten what life is all about.

Can you imagine what it's like to be loved by the Inventor of love? The One who dreamed it all up? God is the Inventor of father-daughter love, mother-son love, brother-brother love, parent-child love, husband-wife love, friend-to-friend love, even boy-to-dog love! He invented them all.

And the Inventor says, "I love *you*! Will you receive it?"

Chapter 9

Trembling at His Faithfulness

There are few things more tragic in the Bible than when God's people refused to trust Him.

And probably nothing more beautiful than when they did.

Think of all the stories that teeter on the razor-edge between belief and unbelief. Remember the ten spies? Because of their unwillingness to trust God, they so influenced the nation that it ended up wandering in the wilderness for forty years. An entire generation lost their way and perished in the sands of the Sinai. Contrast that account with Elijah on Mount Carmel confronting the prophets of Baal. What unflagging confidence in God!

One of the best things God ever did to encourage us to trust Him was to provide us with so many stories—dramatic accounts of prayers answered . . . prophecies fulfilled . . . faith rewarded. In a chapter focusing on God's faithfulness, then, it would seem logical to walk our way through a few of those stories so we might become charged with fresh confidence in God.

But we're not going to do that.

We're going to take a much different journey.

We are going to walk through a long dark tunnel with a man who went to his death with dreams unfulfilled. A man with enough evidence to convince any jury that his God had failed him. Yet a

man who was the inspiration for one of the most famous hymns of
Christendom, "Great Is Thy Faithfulness."

Jeremiah was only a young man—too young, as far as he was
concerned. But God called him to be His prophet during one of
the darkest crises in Jewish history.

> Behold, I have put My words in your mouth.
> See, I have appointed you this day over the nations
>   and over the kingdoms,
> To pluck up and to break down,
> To destroy and to overthrow,
> To build and to plant.
>
> (Jeremiah 1:9-10)

Then, as if to remove all fear and to assure the prophet's success,
God adds,

> Now, behold, I have made you today as a fortified city, and as a pillar
> of iron and as walls of bronze against the whole land. . . . And they
> will fight against you, but they will not overcome you, for I am with
> you to deliver you. (1:18-19)

A tough job? Yes, but with such full divine protection plus guaran-
teed deliverance, he couldn't lose . . . or could he?

In the years that followed, Jeremiah would experience imprison-
ments, beatings, loneliness (he was forbidden to marry), rejection,
attempted assassinations, public ridicule, and—most painful of all—
the apparent failure of God's faithfulness.

> Why has my pain been perpetual
> And my wound incurable, refusing to be healed?
> Wilt Thou indeed be to me like a deceptive stream
> With water that is unreliable? (15:18)

"This I Recall to Mind . . ."

Project yourself back to the critical crossroad of faith in the life
of this man. In the book of Lamentations, Jeremiah has just lived
through the siege and fall of Jerusalem. It lasted a year and a half—
eighteen hellish months that must have seemed like a decade. Food
ran out. Water was scarce. Thousands starved. Disease ran wild.
Mothers cannibalized their own babies.

The hands of compassionate women
Boiled their own children;
They became food for them.

(Lamentations 4:10)

Jeremiah himself was despised, branded as a traitor, tortured for declaring the Word of God.

And then it was over. The temple destroyed. The city—dead. According to Jewish tradition, Jeremiah, now literally skin and bones, sat on the slopes of the Mount of Olives, overlooking the devastation of his once beautiful city: the city of David, the capital of Solomon's glory, the queen of the kingdoms. With tears streaming down his gaunt, deeply creased face, he wrote,

How lonely sits the city
That was full of people!
She has become like a widow
Who was once great among the nations! . . .
She weeps bitterly in the night,
And her tears are on her cheeks. (1:1-2)

As you read the first couple of chapters you hear the prophet saying over and over again, "God, *You* did this! It wasn't just Babylon. You did it!" Then in chapter three his thoughts turn inward. "And not only did You do it to the city, You did it to *me*—to me, Your servant."

He has caused my flesh and my skin to waste away,
He has broken my bones.
He has besieged and encompassed me
    with bitterness and hardship
In dark places He has made me dwell,
Like those who have long been dead . . . .

Even when I cry out and call for help,
He shuts out my prayer. . . .

He has filled me with bitterness,
He has made me drunk with wormwood.
And He has broken my teeth with gravel;
He has made me cower in the dust.
And my soul has been rejected from peace;
I have forgotten happiness.

Then he says,

> So I say, "My strength has perished,
> And so has my hope from the LORD.
>
>   (Lamentations 3:4-16)

Note what he is saying. *God, I'm through with You! It's over! I have no hope in You at all. You say You care for me? You don't! That You would deliver me? You haven't. I can't trust You anymore.*

Have you ever felt like that? What do you do?

What did Jeremiah do? Three verses later we read,

> This I recall to my mind,
> Therefore I have hope.
> The LORD's lovingkindnesses indeed never cease,
> For His compassions never fail.
> They are new every morning;
> Great is Thy faithfulness.
> "The LORD is my portion," says my soul.
> "Therefore I have hope in Him." (3:21-24)

Something happened! Are there some missing verses in the Bible? Did some unrecorded miracle take place that renewed his faith? In three verses we jump from total despair to one of the greatest declarations of faith and confidence and hope in God in all of Scripture.

What happened? Verse 21 holds the key. Jeremiah is saying, "I did something. I recalled something to my mind."

Jeremiah, what did you recall?

"I recalled the Scriptures to my mind . . . what God had said."

Perhaps it was Psalm 136, where in twenty-six verses the phrase "His lovingkindness is everlasting" occurs twenty-six times. Or maybe it was one of dozens of other places in the Scriptures of his day. Jeremiah simply affirmed what the Bible said.

"This I remember, Lord," the prophet trembles as he speaks, "You say that your lovingkindnesses never cease . . . that your compassions never fail . . . that they are new every morning. Lord, *You say that.*" (He's on his knees now. His face is buried in his hands.) "I affirm what You say. I affirm it even though all the evidence around me says it isn't true. It *is* true. You love me. You are God; You cannot lie. Therefore I have hope."

Lamentations from Nooksack

Hymnwriter Thomas Chisholm based the words to "Great Is Thy Faithfulness" on this part of Lamentations. But at one point Chisholm makes an error in his representation of the passage. Remember the chorus?

Great is Thy faithfulness!
Great is Thy faithfulness!
Morning by morning, new mercies I see. . . .

The point is, Jeremiah did *not* see. He didn't see a thing! He had no visible evidence of God's mercies at all. Morning by morning brought horror, pain, and dread, but not "new mercies." Jeremiah could not say "I trust You because I understand it all—because I've got it all figured out." He could only say "I trust You because You are God and You cannot lie."

It's in moments like these that we tremble before the Word of God.

One hundred years before, God described this reverent trust as a quality of the kind of person He favors.

But to this one I will look,
To him who is humble and contrite of spirit,
    and who trembles at My word.

(Isaiah 66:2)

You tremble when you are confronted with incomprehensibility! You tremble before a God you can't put in a box. A God you cannot figure out. Promises unfulfilled. Situations that make no sense at all to you. You tremble. You fall to the floor and bury your face in the rug, and say, "Thou art my God!"

My mind flashes to such an encounter in my own life. It was over twenty years ago, not long after I joined the faculty at Multnomah School of the Bible. For at least a year I had been aware of a progressively worsening sense of mental and emotional stress.

Day and night my mind was like an unstoppable squirrel cage of thoughts. Only with prescription tranquilizers could I hope to sleep at all, and then but for a few hours. Apprehension and nameless fears surged through me again and again.

Searching for explanations, I carefully confessed my sins. I pleaded with God. I dug through all the hurting memories I could uncover.

Confronting and then dealing with them, I sought for inner healing that did not come. I followed every other "deliverance" route I knew of, but still no deliverance came.

Finally, I concluded I was going crazy—that I would end up in storage in some mental institution. The thought filled me with dread. I could not imagine any greater shame to my Christian testimony than for me, a Bible teacher, to end up in an asylum. That would seem to make a lie out of everything I had taught. I remember wishing I had some outwardly recognizable physical disease. Then people would understand and sympathize!

That summer I had to fulfill a prior commitment to speak at a high school camp in northern Washington, in the little town of Nooksack. It's one thing to speak at a camp along some beautiful river or the crashing surf or high in the mountains. But Camp Nooksack was none of that. It was just an odd assortment of buildings by a dusty field in the midst of a sleepy town.

Stepping off the Greyhound bus, I could see carloads of arriving high school kids. I wanted to run. I had nothing to say to them. If only I could run and run until I fell from exhaustion. Maybe I would be lucky enough to have a heart attack and die. At least I wouldn't be a disgrace to God anymore. But I had to stay; I had to speak. It was the last place on earth I wanted to be.

Right before I got up to speak on the first night of camp, they all sang the theme song for the week. The words seemed like so much hollow mockery to me.

Nothing is impossible
When you put your trust in God;
Nothing is impossible
When you're trusting in His Word.

Hearken to the voice of God to thee,
"Is there anything too hard for Me?"

So put your trust in God alone,
And rest upon His Word;
For everything, Oh everything,
Yes everything is possible with God!

The song cut through me like a whip. *Why did they have to pick that song? Things ARE impossible! There are no answers! God does not care*. Than I got up to speak. I smiled, said the right words and somehow made it through. Then the next night and the next. The days dragged by—each followed by another sleepless night.

Every chance I had, I hid away in my hot, drab upstairs room. On one of those interminable afternoons, sitting on the floor by the side of my cot, I started browsing through First Peter, stopping at a verse I memorized years before.

"Casting all your cares upon Him, for He careth for you."

There on the bare floor I remember thinking, *That's NOT true. God does not care for me. I don't know why—but He doesn't.*

That was the last straw. Despair washed over me like a sickening wave. There was nothing more to do or say. There was no hope now. Then I remember interrupting my own darkness with a question.

David, who said those words?

I thought for a moment. I knew, but I didn't want to say it. Finally I replied to myself, "God said it."

Well then, David, can God lie?

Again, I didn't want to answer. I realized that if God could lie, there was nothing to anything. There was no reality—at all—anywhere.

Can He?

"No! He cannot lie."

Then David, that verse is true.

I began to sob. And in my crying I remember yelling out, "God! I didn't know it, but I've been calling You a dirty rotten liar over and over again. I believed You only when my experience confirmed You. I'm sorry. No matter what happens, You *do* care for me. Even if I end up in an insane asylum, scraping my fingers on a padded cell, I will still cry out 'YOU CARE FOR ME!'"

I had no comprehension, no answers to my "whys." Nothing made any more sense to me than before. But now I had something to hang on to.

If God said something, then it was true.

And that was enough. For the first time in my life I trembled at the truthfulness of God, and I would never be the same again.

Many months later I discovered that my stress had been linked to a blood sugar problem—something scoffed at in those days. Yet eventually there was treatment and healing and I have rarely felt that kind of apprehension again.

Trembling before God

I'm sure I would cringe if I knew I had to live that period of my life over again. But I will thank God forever for what He taught me. God's Word is true even when my experience screams out that it's a lie. Even when I cannot figure Him out at all—when I cannot say "Oh, now I understand."

As long as you and I bring God down to the level of our own experience and understanding, as long as we feel justified in putting God and His Word on trial, we will never discover the depths of why He is called "Faithful and True."

I wonder what *impossible* fact God is asking you to believe right now. That He loves you? That He's in control? That He forgives—totally?

How about some of those hard, confrontive facts that strike a mortal blow to casual Christianity? *No one can serve two masters. . . . How shall we who died in sin still live in it? . . . You do not belong to the world. . . . Without holiness no one will see the Lord.*

What will we do with such statements from Scripture? Will we rationalize them, or will we believe and tremble? We who would cringe at the thought of mocking Scripture by denying its absolute inspiration have become experts at adjusting its meaning to fit our experience, our intellect, our comfort level.

A number of years before Jeremiah's cry of faith, God gave another prophet a glimpse of Jerusalem's impending destruction. Shocked beyond measure, Habakkuk tried to argue with the Lord. This thing couldn't be . . . it didn't fit his concept of his God. And then he heard God say,

> Behold, as for the proud one,
> His soul is not right within him;
> But the righteous will live by his faith.
>
> (Habakkuk 2:4)

Realizing that his only right choice was to affirm that God's ways were just and true—even though he had scarcely begun to comprehend them—Habakkuk raised his tear-streaked face to heaven and sang the most agonizing, most joyous song he had ever sung.

Though the fig tree should not blossom,
And there be no fruit on the vines,
Though the yield of the olive should fail,
And the fields produce no food,
Though the flock should be cut off from the fold,
And there be no cattle in the stalls,
Yet I will exult in the LORD,
I will rejoice in the God of my salvation. (3:17-18)

Chapter 10

The Supreme Scientist

It may have started when I saw Andromeda.

Andromeda . . . just a soft, fuzzy glow amid sparkling stars. A bit of luminescent lint on the night sky. A faint fleck of untwinkling light that you could easily miss if you didn't know exactly where to look.

I'd seen it many times before. Amateur astronomy has been a hobby of mine for years—taking long walks at night, locating constellations, pondering the movements of stars and planets across the heavens, and simply allowing myself to be swept up in a sense of wonder. Often I found myself overwhelmed to think that the God who spoke the starry host into being knew me by name—loved me.

On this particular night, however, I felt troubled by what I saw. The vastness weighed on my spirit. The depths and distances overwhelmed me.

I knew that everything I could see in that night sky was part of our own Milky Way, a galaxy of a hundred billion suns and measureless mysteries. Everything, that is, with the exception of that one spot of fuzz high overhead.

A faraway star you might say. Far away, yes. But it isn't a star. Andromeda is our nearest neighboring *galaxy*—an island universe of incomprehensible billions of stars.

But what a mockery to call it a "neighbor." How far would I have to go to visit this neighbor? Let's see. If I could travel at the speed of light—fast enough to make thirty-seven round trips across the United States in a single second—I would shoot past the moon in a second and a half, and past the sun in eight minutes. Before my first day was over I would be out of our solar system, beyond the lonely orbits of Neptune and Pluto. Four years later I might pass the nearest star. Ten thousand years later (give or take a few thousand) I would leave our own galaxy.

How much longer, then, traveling at the speed of light through intergalactic darkness, would it take me to arrive at our neighbor's doorstep?

Two million years.

And what is Andromeda? Part of a little galaxy cluster of which Andromeda and our Milky Way are simply two of a half dozen or so galaxies. And how many *clusters* are there in the universe? Untold millions.

I felt so small that night as I stood in the darkened street. So utterly, microscopically insignificant.

What, after all, is this earth? Just a speck within a speck of an almost endless universe. What kind of God must He be to have produced all this out of infinite nothingness with simply a word? What a fool I was to believe I was of any significance to Him!

Wasn't it rather brash of me to teach my students that mankind was important enough for God to give us His Word and His Son? Wasn't it ridiculously presumptuous for Christians to think we could be at the very center of God's attention?

A Heretical Discovery

In Galileo's day, earth's central position in God's plans presented no intellectual or theological problems at all. Earth was central because it *was* central. The very bull's-eye of the universe. Everyone knew that the sun—and all other heavenly bodies—circled the earth. Any simpleton could stand in the doorway of his home and watch it happen.

"God so loved the world" . . . ? Of course He did! The earth was at the heart of everything. Everything else was peripheral. Why *shouldn't* He?

But then early scientists such as Galileo threatened to spoil everything. It was, Galileo said, becoming increasingly clear that the sun did not—could not—revolve around the earth. In fact it was precisely the *opposite*. The sun was the center of things and the earth was but one of a number of planets making regular, observable revolutions around that center. Galileo had all the figures and calculations he needed to prove it.

The Pope was impressed. So impressed that he put the astronomer under house arrest and threatened him with excommunication if he did not immediately recant and renounce this heresy. It was no idle threat. If you believed in the spiritual authority of Rome, you believed it was within the Primate's power to bind you hand and foot and cast you into the lake of fire for all eternity.

In terror for his soul, Galileo recanted, though he knew in his heart the truth would someday become common knowledge. Now it has, and it is much more startling, much more humbling, than the old astronomer could have ever dreamed.

Imagine with me for a moment that we are able to travel to the nearest star—and then look back toward home. Even if we could look through the most powerful telescope in existence, you and I would never see our planet earth—we wouldn't have the faintest idea it was there.

We're that small.

And we say—the Bible says—that this single grain of sand on an endless shore is the centerpiece of God's purposes? That the Son of God—the very One who spoke this universe into being—would die for us who live on this speck of sand? That doesn't make any sense.

I wrestled with those thoughts as I walked that night. I felt a surge of fear that it would *never* make any sense. Could the Bible be wrong? As I tried to step back and see the flow of the whole Bible through to its final chapter, an analogy came to mind.

The Mystery

Try to imagine God as a scientist. An inventor, creator, designer, engineer. He would, naturally, be the greatest of all scientists—the Supreme Scientist.

This Scientist can create anything. To pursue His experiments and studies He has created a vast science center—the Complex—on thousands of square miles of rolling hills, plains, and deserts. The buildings and laboratories stretch on and on, beyond numbering, beyond calculation. Housed within them are great cyclotrons, nuclear power plants, mammoth banks of computers, soaring towers, architectural masterpieces, infinite varieties of colors, sounds, and shapes. Nearby, on unbounded tracts of forest and meadowland, new life-forms dance in the golden light of a morning sun that never sets.

The Complex vibrates and thunders and shimmers and sings.

Working throughout this Complex is a huge company of white-cloaked technicians, tireless servants of the Scientist who witness His limitless wisdom and creative power and move at the speed of thought to do His bidding.

From the least to the greatest, every technician knows that the Prime Directive calls for absolute purity in the Complex. No hint of impurity—not even the merest thought of contamination—could be tolerated. These standards, however, are no burden for the technicians, who serve their leader with passionate loyalty and great joy. A perpetual sense of awe sweeps across the great environs like freshening rain—each creative wonder from the hands and heart of the Supreme One seems to exceed the last. Anticipation is always rewarded with greater realization than the most daring technician could have imagined.

But here the story takes an unusual twist. There was a mystery in the Complex . . . a mystery so baffling, so deep, that not one among the numberless hosts of technicians could offer the slightest clue toward its answer, though they ached to know it. For the mystery involved the Supreme Scientist Himself.

Day after day they watched the Scientist leave His other pursuits and walk toward one building—just one out of all the buildings within the sprawling reaches of the Complex. It was an average sort of building, a single galaxy cluster out of all the millions of clusters He had made.

Soon there wasn't a technician throughout the whole realm—for news traveled rapidly—who wasn't familiar with the Scientist's strange obsession. He would always walk to exactly the same spot—

into that one ordinary building, through the halls, past many door-
ways until just past a door marked "ANDROMEDA" He would
walk into the room designated "MILKY WAY."

Inside this room were long rows of translucent cabinets filled
with trays of billions of glass slides. Every day, without exception,
the Scientist would walk down the aisles to one cabinet marked
"ORION ARM." Then to one particular drawer which He would
pull open. And finally to one particular glass slide. Just one, with
the tiny label, "Solar System."

Then He would take that all-too-common-looking slide over to
His electron microscope and begin to move it around. He would
see the sun within that slide, but move quickly past it. Jupiter and
Saturn would come into view, but the Scientist would hurry past
these as well, all the while boosting the magnification of His massive
microscope, until . . . a tiny bluish-green speck came into view.

A planet called Earth.

All the massive army of technicians was aware that He would
spend hours looking at that one bit of blue-green on that one tiny
slide from the one file drawer, from the one bank of files, in the one
room of the one building among the mind-staggering millions of
buildings within the Complex.

Why?

The Scientist only added to the perplexity of His technicians
when He told them to pay attention to two infinitesimally small
creatures on the face of that bluish-green speck—two thinking, moving, feeling creatures. "Watch carefully, My servants," He told them.
"What happens with these creatures will be the greatest exhibition
of My creative capacity. The ultimate expression of My greatness."

The Supreme Scientist also informed them that by some process
known only to Him, He had placed *something of Himself* in those
beings. In fact, He had created them in His very image.

Wonders and more wonders! The technicians were reduced to
astonished silence. To think that anything *so small* . . .

The Scientist in His wisdom had also developed a means of
communicating with the creatures—of actually introducing
thoughts from His infinite mind into the minuscule world of their
own minds. He spoke in their language. They could hear His very

voice. They could hear the sound of Him in their garden in the cool of the day.

Day after day the technicians witnessed this most incredible of relationships, as the Supreme Scientist visited with the little ones on the tiny bluish-green speck.

Though no one would have thought of questioning the Scientist's activities, it was . . . well, difficult to comprehend. The technicians were aware—and only partially aware at that—of the length and breadth and multiplied marvels of the Complex. So many wondrous happenings in so many laboratories and galleries and observatories throughout the Scientist's realm—the terror and beauty and glory of it all! Rivers of music . . . mountains of living crystal . . . cathedral caverns of pure color . . . sky-rending explosions of joy . . . all this! Yet the Scientist spent *so much time* with that speck. That one all-but-invisible speck.

Contamination!

The creative years sped by as the Complex remained alive with motion and discoveries and celebrations and a great deal of hard work by the technicians.

When the news came, it fell over the Complex like a sudden shadow. An unspeakable tragedy had taken place. Something inconceivable, monstrous.

Contamination had been discovered within the Supreme Scientist's domain! There was no need of sirens or alarm bells. The Scientist's grief was a tangible presence that could be felt in every corner of the Complex. To make matters worse, the impurity had been discovered in that one building, in the one corridor, in the one room, on the one slide . . . on the tiny bluish-green speck. The very object of the Scientist's prime concern! Some dreadful, incurable virus had somehow enveloped the two tiny creatures. And as the creatures multiplied—the contamination multiplied too. The whole population was dreadfully marked by this vile thing called "sin."

It would only be a matter of time. All the technicians knew what had to be done. The Scientist could not live with impurity—the speck had to be destroyed. He would take a bottle of sulfuric acid, draw out a microscopic portion, and let the droplet fall on the diseased speck. In just an instant it would fume and froth and boil and that would be the end of it. It was unfortunate, but it had to be done. The Prime Directive demanded it. The very purity and integrity of the whole Complex was at stake.

Why then did the Scientist seem to . . . hesitate? The technicians looked at one another as they pursued their many tasks. What was it they felt in the air? A sense of foreboding. An inexplicable feeling that something—an incredible something—was about to happen.

And it did.

The Plan

It began when the Scientist called His Son into the galaxy room of the Milky Way. Word was out that They had talked through one long day and far into the night. They had conceived a plan—a final solution to the contamination dilemma. Yes, the virus would be utterly destroyed. That much had been obvious from the start. The wrath of the Scientist would certainly fall. The deadly sulfuric acid would do its work. But not in the way all the technicians had supposed. Not in a way anyone could have ever imagined.

Was there any limit to this Scientist's power? Did He ever do anything in "the expected way"? Which of the wisest of the technicians could have predicted a plan that would involve *shrinking* the Scientist's own dearly-loved Son down to the size of that diseased speck? And no—more than that—down to the size of one of those infinitely tiny contaminated creatures.

His own Son! His equal in power and wisdom and dignity. The technicians had known the Son from the time of their first awareness. Now He would become like one of those little ones—or was He actually going to become *one* of them?

The Scientist Himself said very little. He simply invited them to watch.

In the days that followed the technicians found themselves thinking constantly about the drama unfolding on the microbe called Earth. A number of them had been permitted to watch in amazement as the Scientist's Son willingly laid aside all His robes and all the vestiges of His authority and honor—and shrank down, down, down until he was lost from sight on the thin glass plate. Still others were allowed to accompany Him on His journey, and bits of strange stories came back about songs on a dark night, a lonely village, and some workmen on the hillsides called shepherds. (How the technicians longed to know more!)

Much later they would sing the stories of the Supreme Son in the days of His smallness. They would speak of how He lived among the diseased ones and ate their food and drank their wine. Of how He shared their joys and their sorrows. They would speak in hushed tones of the day when the Scientist drew the Son aside from the rest and caused all the ghastly filth and contamination of the whole planet to be absorbed into His body.

It would be called The Black Day forever, for who could forget how the Supreme Scientist drew out a measure of the white-hot acid and in great wrath dropped it on His own Son? The scream from the tiny slide could be heard in every corner of the Scientist's realm—*"My God, My God! Why have You forsaken Me?"* Those who witnessed it said the Son burned and foamed and wrenched and died.

The End of the Story?

In perfect agreement with the Son of His love, the Supreme Scientist called once more on His awesome power—for what He would do next would surpass all that He had done before. Calling Him back from the far side of eternal destruction, the Father restored His Son to all His former glory, exalted far, far above the blue-green speck on the glass slide.

In the days that followed, the technicians were aware that from time to time the Scientist would reach down into that slide with infinitesimally small tweezers and pick up those human creatures who had responded to His love. With deep joy He would lift them tenderly from the disease-damaged slide to a new, golden slide—clean and fresh, where no sin, suffering, or sorrow could ever come again.

And that is the end of the story.

Or is it?

Many of us would put a period right there. What happens when you become a Christian? Well, you trust Jesus and you go to heaven when you die and you live happily ever after.

So here I am, one of those atom-sized creatures on a dustspeck planet in a vast universe. And for my sake Almighty God sent His own Son to suffer the very pangs of death and hell—unutterable torture—just so I could be transferred from one little glass slide onto another, far better one.

It's astonishing . . . it's wonderful . . . *but does it really make sense?* Is the cost Christ paid—and what a cost!—worthy of the result? Just so He could transfer a bunch of those creatures from a dirty place to a clean place, so they can skip around happily and strum harps forever? Is it really worth it? Is this the ultimate purpose of this Supreme Scientist, in keeping with His own awesome greatness?

The Bible says, "No! There is more! Much more."

"What Is Man?"

In the Bible, the writer of Hebrews wrestles with questions about man's destiny, his place in God's scheme. He quotes a perplexed David, who wrote: "What is man that You are mindful of him, or the son of man that You take care of him?" (2:6 NKJV).

Can you visualize this young shepherd, stretched out on a grassy Judean hillside beneath the star-studded sky, asking the same question another David (Needham) would be asking three thousand years later?

When I consider Your heavens, the work of Your fingers,
The moon and the stars, which You have ordained,
What is man that You are mindful of him?
(Psalm 8:3-4 NKJV)

Why do you care about us God? Why are we important to You? What is man? You could create throngs of us with just the snap of Your finger! Or You could wipe us out and start off with a whole new batch. Why are You concerned about little man that You would remember him?

David is awed by the thought that God has placed everything on earth under man's rule. Flocks and herds, birds of the air, beasts of the forest, creatures of the sea.

The writer of Hebrews, however, carries this thought a gigantic step further.

He writes, "In putting everything under him [man], God left *nothing* that is not subject to him" (2:8 NIV). A day will come when everything in all creation—even the angelic beings—will fall under the rule of redeemed men and women. Although "at present we do not see everything subject to [man]" (2:8 NIV), God has given us a glimpse of what is to come. The writer tells us that "we see Jesus, who was made a little lower than the angels, now crowned with glory and honor because he suffered death, so that by the grace of God he might taste death for everyone" (2:9 NIV).

The writer goes on to say that this One who ascends into glory *does not go alone.* He brings "many sons to glory" along with Him!

Pick up that same thought in Romans 8. Here we are told the staggering truth that "the Spirit himself testifies with our spirit that we are God's children. Now if we are children, then we are heirs—heirs of God and co-heirs with Christ" (8:16-17 NIV).

Can we begin to imagine what is involved in this? "Co-heirs with Christ"! In fact, verse 19 says that this destiny is so stupendous that "the whole creation is on tiptoe to see the wonderful sight of the sons of God coming into their own" (Phillips). It is as though all of creation—including the technicians/angels—is forming a great audience breathlessly waiting before a curtain-shrouded stage. Soon the last human being to respond to God's grace will arrive. When that happens God will pull the curtain and the audience's holy hush will become one great, reverberating gasp sweeping across the universe as they see "the glory of the children of God" (verse 21).

Peter tells us the technicians are fascinated by God's gracious acts toward you and me—"things into which angels long to look" (1 Peter 1:12). It is not as though they have never seen the power and majesty and artistry of God displayed in an infinite number of ways. Just think of the millions of individually painted sunsets taking place every moment of every day across the globe—every second there is another sunset, with no two the same. And though we see only the sunsets of earth, the angels must witness the setting of a trillion suns over planets beyond number—over fantastic landscapes no human eye has ever seen.

Yet these who behold God's throne and the wonders of the universe are *consumed with longing* to delve into the mystery of God's grace toward man. They have seen the artistry and creativity of God—they're used to that. But they have never seen nor imagined how God could take something so small and by His sheer divine power transform it into something so glorious.

The miracle of the Supreme Scientist, then, is not just that He got us out of a terrible mess in order to transfer us to a clean environment. That's not big enough!

He not only rescued us—He has made us His very sons and daughters.

He not only made us His sons and daughters—He has placed us over His whole creation.

He not only placed us over His whole creation—He has made us joint-heirs to all that belongs to the Son of God.

And He not only made us joint heirs with His Son . . . He is in the process—even now—of doing something even more astonishing.

The Father Seeks a Bride

Long into the night, hour after hour, the Scientist and His Son discussed the Son's upcoming departure for the tiny planet Earth. During those hours the Scientist set forth His plans and purposes. Might the Supreme Scientist have used words like these?

"So you see, My Son, My purpose is not only to rescue these little ones from contamination and death, but also to transform them through Your death and resurrection into My own sons and daughters—co-heirs of everything I have given to You. And even beyond that, My Son, when it's all over, I'm going to gather them up as one, and present them to You as Your eternal *bride*.

"Your bride, My Son! You're going down there to that infinitesimal speck to bring back Your bride!"

In teaching about marriage in his letter to the Ephesians, Paul wrote: "Christ loved the church and gave himself up for her to make her holy, cleansing her by the washing with water through the word, and to present her to himself as a radiant church, without stain or wrinkle or any other blemish, but holy and blameless" (5:25-27 NIV). A few lines later he adds, "This is a profound mystery—but I am talking about Christ and the church" (5:32 NIV).

Paul is saying, "Listen carefully, Ephesians. This isn't simply a lesson on husband-wife relationships. I'm giving you a glimpse into one of the greatest mysteries in the universe! The ultimate destiny for a Christian is to know an intimacy with Jesus forever—for which the nearest human analogy is the warm, secure, delightful bond between a man and a woman. Jesus Christ is a bridegroom—*and you are the bride!"*

It's hard to even imagine. The moment will come when these humble bodies will be transformed to be like the glorified body of Jesus Christ. The moment will come when the Son of God will take His church—collectively, almost as one person—to be His eternal bride. And all the technician angels will bow before their Master and marvel that this masterpiece of grace is worthy of the God they have known for ages.

If a great Scientist took something great in itself and made it greater, that would be remarkable. But if that Scientist took something thoroughly impure, infinitely small, and utterly insignificant and transformed it into something gloriously pure and great beyond comprehension . . . *that* would be an act worthy of His greatness. *That* would be something to sing about for eternity.

Then I heard what sounded like a great multitude, like the roar of rushing waters and like loud peals of thunder, shouting:
"Hallelujah!
For our Lord God Almighty reigns.
Let us rejoice and be glad
and give him glory!
For the wedding of the Lamb has come,
and his bride has made herself ready.
Fine linen, bright and clean,
was given her to wear."
(Revelation 19:6-8 NIV)

This is our future. This is reality. Perhaps in the busy activities of daily living, we've lost sight of it. And somehow holiness has become legalism. And Scriptures become academic. And Christian life becomes duty. God never meant it to be like that! He has given us a glimpse of a destiny so awesome, so mind-boggling that daily living can be infused with wonder and praise.

On the Way Home

I finished my night walk under the stars and paused at the front steps of my home. The little allegory of the Scientist, weak as it was, filled my heart with awe.

Does it make sense that God would choose an insignificant someone like me on a lonely little dustspeck in a far corner of His wide, wide universe?

Yes, it does. His eternal glory is fulfilled in my destiny.

You and I are on our way to a wedding. Our wedding. The Groom is waiting on the steps . . . but the road before us is muddy and filled with holes.

May God help us to walk carefully.

Chapter 11

Does God Need Me?

Way back before the beginning, when there was just God—no people, no angels, just God—what was it like?

Jesus gives us two hints in that wondrous prayer to His Father in John 17.

And now, O Father, glorify Me together with Yourself, with the glory I had with You before the world was.

. . . for You loved Me before the foundation of the world. (17:5 and 17:24 NKJV)

Always, before the beginning of anything, there was love, there was glory, there was togetherness—between God the Father, His Son, and the Holy Spirit.

Why then, since everything must have been perfect, did God ever "start" us? Did He need us? Does He need me?

The fiftieth psalm would appear to answer "No." Almost with a degree of humor God says,

If I were hungry, I would not tell you;
For the world is Mine, and all it contains. (50:12)

It's as though God were saying, "Listen, do you think I would bother you if I had some need? As though I somehow depend on you to keep Me going?"

No, God does not need us. If all the world ceased to believe in God, that would not damage Him at all. My belief does not make Him more, nor would my unbelief make Him less. Would the sun cease to shine if the entire world signed a petition claiming that it did not exist? No, it would continue to rise in the morning, shine on meadow and stream and forest, and set in the evening. It would continue to blaze through the black fields of space along its determined route. The sun simply is—whether I acknowledge it or not.

You and I are like little ponds of water that exist only because tiny rivulets of life pour into us. God is like a lofty ocean, above which there is nothing higher to flow into Him at all. He simply is. The apostle Paul writes, "Neither is He served by human hands, as though He needed anything, since He Himself gives to all life and breath and all things" (Acts 17:25).

"I Want to Be Needed"

Thoughts such as these used to trouble me. After all, I wanted to be needed—not just by people, but by God. We who love Him want to think that we somehow are fulfilling something for Him. I wondered hard about that, especially when I remembered a certain evening years ago when I was in high school.

Among the things we grew on our ranch in southern California were some twenty-five acres of lemon trees. On this particular day I had been irrigating those trees—hot, hard, dusty work. All day long I had nudged the water down dozens of clogged furrows, dug out gopher holes, and set and reset the water volume. By early evening the irrigation at last was flowing smoothly, ready to run on through the night.

Leaning on my shovel, I looked across the terraced hillside, down the long San Luis Rey Valley and out to the open sea beyond. As I stood there drinking it all in, I began to realize I was in for a special treat. The way the clouds were gathering and the colors deepening, I knew that before long I would be gazing on one of those "once in a long time" masterpiece sunsets.

Suddenly I found myself running as fast as I could—leaping ditches, cutting up terraces, pushing through the branches. Coming finally to the end of the orchard I sprinted through the sage brush and mesquite just below our home on the hilltop. Crossing the driveway and lunging through the back door, I grabbed my startled mother by the arm.

"Mom!"

My breath came in ragged gasps. "Mom! You've . . . got to see."

Too out of breath to say anything more, I half dragged her to the big picture window at the west end of our living room.

"Mom . . . look!"

With my arm around her, we stood in silence as the sky glowed with vivid colors that gradually changed and finally gave way to gathering darkness.

Did I need her to see the sunset? No. I could have watched it perfectly well by myself down among the trees. But something in me wanted someone else. Someone to watch with me. Someone who might have missed it all had I watched it alone.

I wonder. Could this be one of the reasons God reached down to people like you and me? Does He need me? No. And yet . . . I wonder.

In His infinite knowledge God is aware not only of the magnificent glory of every facet of His being, but also of the endless dimensions of His own creativity. Having all of it seen, delighted in, and shared only within the Godhead perhaps was not enough. Somehow He *chose* to need us! He chose to want us.

He has given us eternal life in Christ, Paul says,

> that in the ages to come He might show the exceeding riches of His grace in His kindness toward us in Christ Jesus. (Ephesians 2:7 NKJV)

Listen again to Jesus pray:

> Father, I desire that they also whom You gave Me may be with Me where I am, that they may behold My glory which You have given Me; for You loved Me before the foundation of the world . . . that the love with which You loved Me may be in them, and I in them. (John 17:24-26 NKJV)

What mystery! A God so vast, so beyond, so incomprehensible—somehow wants me! And He wants you. This very fact underlines something else, too. God's message of forgiveness—of life and hope for the human race—is more than simply a proposition to be accepted or rejected. It is rather an offer of a love relationship to be enjoyed or to be forfeited.

For this to be so requires something we easily take for granted. Our God is a genuine, full-fledged *Person*. He is far more than "the Force," or "Love," or any other *thing*—He is a Person who relates to us personally. Listen to part of a very familiar story.

> I will get up and go to my father, and will say to him, "Father, I have sinned against heaven, and in your sight; I am no longer worthy to be called your son; make me as one of your hired men." And he got up and came to his father. But while he was still a long way off, his father saw him, and felt compassion for him, and ran and embraced him, and kissed him. (Luke 15:18-20)

The prodigal son is you and I—the father is God. It is God who "embraced and kissed" us! Of course if He had done it physically when we turned to Him, it would have scared us to death. But He did do it! Could His personhood be sketched in any plainer way?

Near the close of the Bible John records one of the most intimate, tender expressions of God's personal relationship with us:

> And I heard a loud voice from the throne, saying, "Behold, the tabernacle of God is among men, and He shall dwell among them, and they shall be His people, and God Himself shall be among them, and He shall wipe away every tear from their eyes." (Revelation 21:3-4)

I can't think of anything that expresses the love and tenderness we feel toward our young children more than this act of wiping away tears. At this very moment I can look back over the years and see my little daughter running to me with tears streaming down her face. Squeezing her close, I would gently wipe away those tears with my hand. And wipe and wipe until at last the tears were gone.

God will not delegate any "tear wiping" committee when we arrive in heaven. No! "He Himself . . . shall wipe away every tear." He is my—your—*personal* Savior.

In light of this profound yet most intimate truth, how important it is that you and I respond to Him personally!

"Just a Few Words, Lord"

Most of us have read with envy the various biblical accounts of God speaking directly, audibly, with His people. And of course He could still choose to speak in such a way any time He wishes. Yet I have never heard His audible voice. Most likely you haven't, either.

However, since we know the Bible *is* His voice, let's imagine the next time you are reading your Bible. Suddenly you recognize that your circumstance is essentially the same as that of the people you are reading about. Could God possibly be saying to you the same thing He said to them? Of course He is! Because God does not change, and the circumstance is the same.

Perhaps right now you are wondering whether God has forgotten all about you. It hurts to feel that way, doesn't it? Has God anything to say to you—right now? He does! Remember that you are feeling exactly how Israel felt so long ago.

> But Zion said, "The LORD has forsaken me, and the Lord has forgotten me."

God answers,

> Can a woman forget her nursing child,
> And have no compassion on the son of her womb?
> Even these may forget, but I will not forget you.
> Behold, I have inscribed you on the palms of My hands;
> Your walls are continually before Me.
> (Isaiah 49:14-16)

God *is* saying these very words to you—now. I do not believe we misuse Scripture when we put ourselves into God's response:

> Even these may forget, but I will not forget you, David.
> I have inscribed you, David, on the palms of My hands.
> Not just your name, David, but *you*.

Yes, God is actually speaking those words to me, as truly as if I heard His voice. In fact, why not let your voice *be* His as you personalize those promises you know are yours to claim? When no one else is around, take a verse you know is for you and speak it out loud, inserting your name. Hear Him speaking to you. It is not by chance that we call the Bible "The Word of God."

Yet what about those times when no Scripture seems to fit? We may not be quite sure what God would wish to say to us.

One night after our children had gone to bed, I was out walking and talking with God (a practice that has become more precious to me than I can ever say). This particular night I found myself wishing

God would speak audibly to me—something He had never done before. I was just beginning my teaching career at Multnomah School of the Bible. The preceding day had gone well enough, but for some reason I felt I needed God's stamp of approval on my work. Was He satisfied with what I was teaching about Him?

If only He would clear the air! It would be so simple for Him to speak.

"Just a few words, Lord."

I stopped walking. I listened.

"Father, I won't talk at all—I'll simply wait, just in case You have something to say."

There was no answer. Nothing but the ever-present hum of the city. Though I'm not quite sure just what I had expected to happen that night, I remember turning home with a heavy heart. Was God pleased with my service? I really didn't know.

The next morning I found attached to my office door not just one or two, but a dozen individual notes from my students. As I read them I began to cry. For each note was an expression of thanks to God for things I had shared with them in class the day before. That never happened before or since!

Could it be that my God had personalized Himself through them? The assurance of that fact flooded my spirit in an instant.

He is a Person. He has chosen to need us, not simply for service, but to love and be loved. To share a closeness of relationship that will take an eternity to fulfill. Yet He has also chosen us (just like those dozen students) from time to time to be His personal voice to someone who needs that word from God. What a wonderful privilege! May we be sensitive and available.

Most of the time, for now, "we walk by faith." Soon, by sight.

> For now we see in a mirror dimly, but then face to face; now I know in part, but then I shall know fully just as I also have been fully known. (1 Corinthians 13:12)

Ours is a personal God who has chosen to need us. There are countless sunsets He has yet to share with us. Our Friend the Artist beckons us to the window.

Chapter 12

In the Circle of His Love

It is the most perfect, most beautiful love story in the universe.

God's love for you and me?

No—even more wondrous than that, if such a thing could be.

Stand with me on the banks of the Jordan River. Watch. A young man wades out into the swirling, muddy waters. Another young man, his face awash with conflicting currents of disapproval and wonder, stands in the flowing water, waiting. The first bids the second to plunge him beneath the water . . .

> And immediately, coming up from the water, He saw the heavens parting and the Spirit descending upon Him like a dove. Then a voice came from heaven, "You are My beloved Son, in whom I am well pleased." (Mark 1:10-11 NKJV)

You are My *beloved* Son. You are the Son I love.

Not since the angels announced His birth to the shepherds had there been one public word from heaven concerning the miracle baby . . . the little boy of Nazareth . . . the young carpenter . . . the supposed illegitimate son of Mary. Over thirty years of silence. And then "the heavens were opened."

But why those particular words?

Couldn't He have said simply, "You're My Son," and in that

announce to all who were there the unique identity of that Person coming up out of the Jordan? Yet He chose to say more.

Look ahead now a few years from that moment. The Lord Jesus and three of His men pick their way up a steep hillside. Suddenly

> He was transfigured before them. His clothes became shining, exceedingly white, like snow, such as no launderer on earth can whiten them . . . And a cloud came and overshadowed them; and a voice came out of the cloud, saying, "This is My beloved Son. Hear Him!" (Mark 9:2 and 9:7 NKJV)

Hear Me, Peter, James, and John. *This is the One I love.* Listen to Him!

Perhaps reflecting on that very moment with his Lord Jesus, John later wrote,

> For He whom God has sent speaks the words of God; for He gives the Spirit without measure. *The Father loves the Son,* and has given all things into His hand. (John 3:34)

Was it necessary for John to mention the Father's love for the Son? After all, the emphasis of John's gospel is that Jesus Christ is the Son of God, and that by believing Him we can find life in His name. He didn't have to comment on this mysterious love-bond within the Trinity. Yet John—and the Holy Spirit—knew that this was crucial truth for you and me to consider and understand.

How did the Son respond to these expressions of love? Did He consider them—delight in them? What did it mean to the Lord Jesus to be so loved by His Father?

We have a strong clue in a parable Jesus told.

> A man planted a vineyard and set a hedge around it, dug a place for the wine vat and built a tower. And he leased it to vinedressers and went into a far country. Now at vintage time he sent a servant to the vinedressers, that he might receive some of the fruit of the vineyard from the vinedressers. And they took him and beat him and sent him away empty-handed. Again he sent them another servant, and at him they threw stones, wounded him in the head, and sent him away shamefully treated. And again he sent another, and him they killed; and many others, beating some and killing some.

> Therefore still having one son, *his beloved,* he also sent him to them last, saying, "They will respect my son."

> But those vinedressers . . . took him and killed him and cast him out of the vineyard (Mark 12:1-8 NKJV)

Jesus, who obviously spoke of Himself and His Father in the parable, knew that He was the "beloved"—the greatly loved son. He was aware of that deep love. It meant something to Him. It was something He mulled over during the days of His humanity on earth. *"My Father loves Me!"*

Finally, at the sunset moments of our Lord's earthly ministry, John pulls back the curtain on the most mysterious, intimate, piercingly beautiful prayer in all the Bible. The Lord Jesus pours out His heart before His Father—and allows the saints of all ages to listen in. Near the end of that prayer, Jesus says:

> Father, I desire that they also whom You gave Me may be with Me where I am, that they may behold My glory which You have given Me, for You loved Me before the foundation of the world. (17:24 NKJV)

"Father," Jesus is saying, "You have loved Me from eternity past. You've given Me glory, Father. *I want them to see it!* Because if they see it, they'll know how much You love Me!"

This is the one reason—at least in this passage—that Jesus gives for desiring us to be in heaven with Him. If we could only have a chance to see the Father's gift to His Son—glory from "before the foundation of the world"—we would understand at last the intensity, the greatness, of His Father's love for Him.

"That the World May Know . . . Let's Go"

But so far in this perfect love story, it sounds as though the love was all one way—the Father loving the Son. Could this be so?

Frankly, I was surprised as I searched through the gospels. I found it difficult to find a passage where Jesus actually affirms His own love for the Father. Then I ran headlong into John 14:30-31. And I realized that for Jesus to express His love for the Father at *that* particular moment in His life was tantamount to saying it a million times over.

It was mere minutes before the crushing agony of Gethsemane. Scarce hours before the horror of the cross. Concluding an upper room conversation with His men, Jesus said:

> I will not speak much more with you, for the ruler of the world is coming, and he has nothing in Me; but that the world may know that I love the Father, and as the Father gave Me commandment, even so I do. Arise, let us go from here.

Go where?

To the cross. To unspeakable torture. To pain and loneliness and humiliation and suffering beyond words—beyond conception.

"Arise, let us go." Let's get on with it. Why? "That the world may know that I love the Father."

Often we are told that the cross reveals how much God loved us. And that's true. But the cross also reveals how much Jesus loved His Father. Every act of obedience to His Father was an affirmation of His love. Are we pressing our imagination too far to hear faint whispers between the stinging lashes of the scourging? "I love You, Father. I love You." Under the crown of thorns, "I love You!" As the nails pierced His flesh, "I love You!"

Centuries before, Isaiah described our Lord's obedience in torturous detail:

> The Lord God has opened my ear;
> And I was not disobedient,
> Nor did I turn back.
> I gave My back to those who strike Me,
> And My cheeks to those who pluck out the beard;
> I did not cover My face from humiliation and spitting.
>
> (Isaiah 50:5-6)

And why? "That the world may know that I love the Father, and as the Father gave Me commandment, even so I do."

Why He Wants Us to Know

Why is it so crucial that you and I consider the depths of love in this eternal Father-Son relationship? One reason, of course, is that it provides us with the ultimate example of love. We are so often overwhelmed by twisted and tarnished pictures of "love," it's good to be able to look up and be reminded that the ideal *does* exist. It's not a fantasy.

But there is a greater answer to this question. One that staggers the imagination. And it is this: God wants us to understand the eternal intimacy He shares with His Son *because this is precisely the kind of love the Father and Son have for you and me.*

That same evening before Gethsemane Jesus said:

> As the Father has loved me, *so* I have loved you. Now remain in my love. (John 15:9 NIV)

Later, as He prayed to His Father, He requested

> that the world may know that Thou didst send Me, and didst love them, *even as* Thou didst love Me. (17:23)

"Even as!" It would seem as though the intimacy of love that exists between Father and Son—so sacred, so pure—should be theirs privately forever. We should be seen as intruders. But no! We are actually invited inside this love. Their love. Each of us is loved by God *that* way.

Completing the Circle

What more could be added to this perfect circle of love? Father-Son. Son-Father. Son and Father—you and I. Yet there *is* more.

> A new commandment I give to you, that you love one another, *even as* I have loved you, that you also love one another. By this all men will know that you are My disciples, if you have love for one another. (John 13:34-35)

> This is My commandment, that you love one another *just as* I have loved you. (15:12)

Clearly the priority of love Jesus has in mind is love between Christians—even eclipsing our concern for the world.

> . . . that they may all be one . . . that the world may believe. (17:21)
> . . . that they may be perfected in unity, that the world may know. (17:23)

A few minutes ago I browsed through the "Churches" section in our local telephone directory yellow pages. What an education! Denominations I had never heard of, plus all the individual groups that rejected any classification. Even if I removed from the list all the church groups that are not "Christian" by any valid measurement, the assortment is still staggering.

Could anything be more fragmented than Christianity? How could we possibly be "perfected in unity"?

It hurts to look directly at a commandment of God I am to obey and hear myself saying, "It can't be done. There's no way Christians can 'be one.' It's impossible. It's a waste of time even to dream."

Well, let's dream anyway.

Let's imagine all the Christians in the churches in your town or city have suddenly been picked up and placed deep inside Albania, home of the most virulent communism in the world. To affirm one's trust in Jesus would be to invite imprisonment or death. What would happen?

First of all, it would be safe to assume the membership rolls of each church would quickly become sprinkled with blank spaces. Not because of death, but because of desertion.

What else would happen? Very quickly, denominational distinctives and pampered pet doctrines would shrivel away. Why? They would be overpowered by the deep sense of value each believer would feel toward the others. Walls of tradition and culture that have divided believers for hundreds of years would tumble. Each believer would become a *treasure*—a priceless commodity to be embraced by the rest of the spiritual family.

Is that really what would happen? Yes—and it's exciting to think about. But since it's not the way things actually *are*, is there a point in dreaming?

Yes, and this is the point: What "would be" is actually "what is." In other words, this imagined change of ours is only a change in *circumstance*, not a change in *people*. What these other believers would be—treasured members of my spiritual family—is what they are today, right now. Whether I recognize it or not.

Think, for example, of one person in your own church with whom you have a difficult time getting along. Then imagine both of you suddenly transported to the middle of a concentration camp. Both of you are to be shot by a firing squad within a few days. You are still the same individuals as you were before, with all your differences. But now those "differences" seem absurdly trivial! They have been swallowed up by the treasured bond you share. You are not alone. You stand together. You will die together.

Can you imagine in that moment trying to change that other person to fit your comfort zone? It would be unthinkable. Why take the slightest chance of quenching the warmth of love to which the two of you cling in those final hours?

All right, we're still dreaming. We are not in concentration camps. We are not facing the muzzle of a Soviet assault rifle. Yet *you and I can make the choice to value persons above circumstances if we want to*—any time we want to.

And we must! Do you remember what is at stake?

. . . that the world may believe . . . that the world may know.

God says our oneness—our unity—will break through the darkness to touch the countless millions He longs to redeem. Could this be one of those long sought-after keys to world evangelization?

If you are committed to taking God seriously, here is a suggestion—though perhaps a dangerous one. Try reading Romans 14:1 through 15:7 every day for a week. Where appropriate, replace the pronouns in the passage with *your own name*. Then begin the difficult process of inserting those verses into the particular issues which right now stand as walls between yourself and those "out of step" brothers and sisters whose lives cross your own. But be careful as you begin applying these truths! You may start a revolution.

A Continuing Miracle

John 17 isn't finished with us yet. It confronts us with yet one more seeming impossibility. The passage tells us that we are to love each other with the *same kind of love* God has for us. How could this be? How can God ask us to love others with a quality of love we don't have? We know what our love is like—so unsteady, so guarded, so often blurred with our own selfishness.

We might despair of such a directive . . . until we read these words:

. . . that the love with which You loved Me may be in them, and I in them . . . I in them, and You in Me; that they may be made perfect in one. (John 17:26 and 17:23 NKJV)

That's it! There could be no other way! Nothing short of a continuing *miracle*. My life, the miracle extension of Jesus' life—of Jesus' love. Perfect love has come to dwell in me because Christ is in me. Not to to stay locked up inside, but to be poured out. Could there be any greater miracle—any greater sign or wonder that would jolt our world more than this? To see, poured out like water on thirsty ground, the love of God for others!

God has commanded us to search out the lowest common denominator that would identify other people as part of the family of God. Having done that, we have no greater command than to love them—to give ourselves to them for their welfare.

"But how much?" you might ask. "How far should this go? If Christ *is* my life, how far should I expect Him to take me in expressing His life and love?"

The answer is not a comfortable one.

We know love by this, that He laid down His life for us; and we ought to lay down our lives for the brethren. (1 John 3:16)

That far?

There is a true story of a little boy whose sister needed a blood transfusion. The doctor explained that she had the same disease the boy had recovered from two years earlier. Her only chance of recovery was a transfusion from someone who had previously conquered the disease. Since the two children had the same rare blood type, the boy was an ideal donor.

"Would you give your blood to Mary?" the doctor asked.

Johnny hesitated. His lower lip started to tremble. Then he smiled and said, "Sure, for my sister."

Soon the two children were wheeled into the hospital room. Mary, pale and thin. Johnny, robust and healthy. Neither spoke, but when their eyes met, Johnny grinned.

As the nurse inserted the needle into his arm, Johnny's smile faded. He watched the blood flow through the tube.

With the ordeal almost over, Johnny's voice, slightly shaky, broke the silence.

"Doctor, *when do I die?*"

Only then did the doctor realize why Johnny had hesitated, why his lip had trembled when he agreed to donate his blood. He thought giving his blood to his sister would mean giving up his life. In that brief moment, he had made his great decision.

My life being poured out to bring healing—oneness—to my fragmented bothers and sisters in Christ all over the world. Nothing less than this will be enough.

But where do I begin?

For most of us, it must begin with a radical reprogramming of our hearts. We must change how we look at our own lives, how we look at our brothers and sisters in Christ . . . and what we believe about miracles.

Chapter 13

Wrath and Grace

So often it's the children who suffer most. The helpless.

Scarcely a news report goes by but I am struck once more with the overwhelming suffering and need across our world. Famines, floods, disease, earthquakes, oppression, perversions, racism, tortures, terrorism, wars . . . where does the list end?

Some tell us that the world struggles on in the darkness because we Christians have failed to be the "salt" and the "light" we were meant to be. That the time has come for Christians to claim the political "clout" their growing numbers deserve. With that power, worldwide healing could take place. Hope could blossom, nature could be tamed, governments transformed, and human suffering dispelled.

If only that were true, we Christians could optimistically pour ourselves into aggressive political action. We could move ahead with confidence knowing that the solutions to the world's hurts were just around the corner. That our light soon would swallow up the darkness.

Yes, we are the salt of the earth and light in the darkness. A city on a hill. Ours is the privilege of reaching out and dispensing the compassion of God to hurting people everywhere. But this does not change the fact that the wrath of God weighs heavy upon this world. The Bible makes it clear that the curse of God upon our planet and its people still remains. Not to mention the fact that Satan, the prince of this world, will not give up his power until forced to by the triumphant return of Christ.

Once again, we are peering into mystery. But this time I am giving you an invitation to hurt with me. To share for a few minutes in my personal struggle of attempting to make some sense out of the agelong enigma of human anguish and divine wrath. Whether "hurt" and "struggle" are the right words, you will have to judge. Yet before we begin, I need to tell you one thing . . . and that is, how we will end. We will end by seeing the grace of God as more glorious, more mind-boggling than perhaps we have ever seen it before.

"Dear God, We Don't Understand . . ."

My first recollection of my hurt—my struggle—came a number of years ago. Mary Jo and I heard the news that widespread flooding had not only killed multitudes in Bangladesh, but had also destroyed countless homes and ravaged thousands of acres of farmlands. The people who survived could not survive for long. Deeply touched, we sent off what to us was a significant gift. There was joy in that—knowing homes would be rebuilt and crops planted once more. Perhaps if others shared, these desperate people could have hope again.

In the months that followed we received word of new wells dug and homes going up. What a warm feeling of satisfaction we felt to have a part in life being restored!

And then it happened all over again.

Floods roared once more through the same area, wreaking worse havoc than before. All that we had given had been swept away. We felt betrayed—by God!

"God, why? You who are the best equipped to do something—You who stilled the seas and fed the hungry and healed the brokenhearted. Yet when the needs were so great in Bangladesh, You stood by and did nothing while we sacrificed and gave. And when hope was beginning to blossom, only to be crushed once more, You continued to do nothing to help. All it would have taken from You was a word—just a word! We reached out to help. But it is almost as though You became our adversary—working against the compassion we thought came from You. Please, dear God, we don't understand!"

Yet my hurting "whys" went even further.

Couldn't God Have Done More?

Paul tells us that God "desires all men to be saved and to come to the knowledge of the truth" (1 Timothy 2:4). Christian leaders remind us that we've been charged with "the great commission." If we fail to share the gospel with those who have not heard, their blood will be upon our hands. And that is true—up to a point.

But what about all the centuries that passed before Christians even knew there was a western hemisphere, not to mention the hundreds of lonely islands in the sea? Dozens of generations passed into eternity, never hearing of Jesus. Are we to blame for that? And what about the thousands of language barriers missionaries struggle with so long? Wasn't God the one who confused those languages to begin with? Does He really care?

I hesitate to even verbalize this next question. It's right at the root of my struggle. *Since God truly loves the world, why has He not chosen a more successful way to show it?*

We know He loved the world—the Cross shouts out that fact. But why all these thousands of years of human anguish? Yes, man is terribly sinful; but couldn't God somehow have done more than He has to ease the long nightmare of history?

Writing these words has been so difficult. I am repelled at the thought of casting the slightest shadow on the compassion, the greatness, and the wonder of our God. Not even for a moment would I suggest that God is on trial.

But the questions are there, aren't they?

And until we are honest enough with ourselves to get them out where we can look at them, they will only fester and grow. Perhaps now we can turn to God's Word for whatever answers He might wish to give us.

God Owes Us Nothing!

The first answer is simply the fact that God does not owe us any answers at all. We don't like that, but it's true. He is the supreme Ruler and we are His subjects. Perhaps the answers He might give would be so majestic, so far beyond our minds to grasp, that as He said to Habakkuk, "You would not believe if you were told."

Also, we must not forget that God is not looking for the person who has the solutions all neatly filed away, but for the one who in humility "trembles" at His Word. Job learned that, didn't he? There was a time in his anguish and confusion when he felt justified in saying,

Even today my complaint is rebellion;
His hand is heavy despite my groaning.
Oh that I knew where I might find Him, . . .
And fill my mouth with arguments.
I would learn the words which He would answer,
And perceive what He would say to me.
Would He contend with me by the greatness of His power?
No, surely He would pay attention to me.

(Job 23:1-6)

Yet when at last God gave him that opportunity to hear His answer, Job responded,

Therefore I have declared that which I did not understand,
Things too wonderful for me, which I did not know.
Therefore I retract,
And I repent in dust and ashes.

(Job 42:3 and 42:6)

God owes us nothing! Yet time and again through the Bible we discover that this God of ours welcomes us to step up close to the mystery of His ways . . . to see just enough to bring us to our knees in worship and wonder. What then does He wish us to see? What answers has He chosen to share with us about this tragic paradox of human anguish?

No Compromise with Sin

To begin with, we must know—if we are ever to know God— something of the intensity of His wrath. His scathing, reverberating repulsion toward everything that is contrary to holiness. Listen . . .

For thus the LORD, the God of Israel, says to me, "Take this cup of the wine of wrath from My hand, and cause all the nations, to whom I send you, to drink it. And they shall drink and stagger and go mad because of the sword that I will send among them."

"And you shall say to them, 'Thus says the LORD of hosts, the God of Israel, "Drink, be drunk, vomit, fall, and rise no more because of the sword which I will send among you." ' "And it will be, if they refuse to take the cup from your hand to drink, then you will say to them, 'Thus says the LORD of hosts: "You shall surely drink!" ' (Jeremiah 25:15-16 and 25:27-28)

Sin must not go unpunished regardless of who has to suffer. In fact, one of sin's most hideous characteristics is that so often its painful effects spread far beyond the individual who commits the sin. Punishment is God's absolute, unbending edict. We might wish this were not so. That He would simply cancel the consequences, forgive and forget.

Why can't He do that, we ask? Since He can choose to do whatever He wills, what stands in His way? His answer lies within God's own integrity—His own perfect purity. His name is "Holy . . . Faithful and True." To compromise would be to violate Himself.

For the wrath of God is revealed from heaven against all ungodliness and unrighteousness of men. (Romans 1:18)

God's necessary curse on both the human race and the earth we walk upon *must* run its course. After the thousands of years since the Fall in the Garden, His curse and His wrath upon sinful men continue unabated. God will not give paradise to a world that rejects His claim to their allegiance.

Shaping the Ashes

Are we then to picture God on His throne, dreaming up the next accident you are going to have, or the next tragically deformed baby to be born, or the next atrocity to be committed? Every time an adversity comes along, is it right to ask God, "Why did *You* do this to me?"

Yes, there are times in the Bible when God *was* directly involved. When ancient Assyria, gloating in their success at crushing Israel, bragged, "By the power of my hand and by my wisdom I did this"—God responds by saying "Yes, you're the ax, but I'm the One

Who swings it; you're the club, but I wield it" (Isaiah 10:13-15, my paraphrase).

Yet certainly the greatest share of human adversity comes as the result of man's failure to reckon with the physical and moral laws God has ordained and energized. If a drunk careening down the road smashes head-on into your son or daughter's car, please don't say to God, "How could You do that to my child?" God deserves no blame for man's misuse of drugs, his body, his environment, and his relationships with others. We have been mocking His physical and moral laws for thousands of years. Man reaps what he sows. Sometimes God may choose to intervene in healing and deliverance, but more often, it would appear, He shares our grief instead.

The amazing thing is that so often God gathers up the ashes of adversity and shapes them for His glory and our good. As a reminder, take a good look the next time you see an exquisite piece of pottery shaped from Mount St. Helen's ash.

"How Long, Lord?"

Finally, though we wish it otherwise, we still live in unredeemed bodies on a cursed planet. This too, God has ordained.

> For we know that the whole creation groans and suffers the pains of childbirth together until now. And not only this, but also we ourselves, having the first fruits of the Spirit, even we ourselves groan within ourselves. (Romans 8:22-23)

But why did God have to allow sin to begin with? Could it be that God has permitted it so that every conceivable alternative to His own perfection might have a chance to come out in the open—demonstrating how black it truly is—and then be judged eternally? Beyond that I do not know why. Early in Genesis, God spoke some strange words to Abraham. They seem to infer that sin too must run its course.

> And as for you, you shall go to your fathers in peace; you shall be buried at a good old age. Then in the fourth generation they shall return here, *for the iniquity of the Amorite is not yet complete*. (15:15-16)

It sounds as though God is suggesting that He would take the descendants of Abraham out of the promised land for a while until the Amorites who lived there had enough time to fully express the evil that was in them.

This same idea may surface in the last book of the Bible, where we find the martyred saints in heaven asking God how much longer it would be until His judgment fell on their executioners.

> And there was given to each of them a white robe; and they were told that they should rest for a little while longer, *until the number* of their fellow servants and their brethren who were to be killed even as they had been, *should be completed* also. (Revelation 6:11)

Satan still is the prince of this world. Someday his iniquity will also be complete. And he and all who share allegiance to him will be cast into the lake of fire forever.

Our initial question, however, still remains: Why didn't God choose "a more successful way" to show His love? Why couldn't His wish for "all men to be saved" come closer to fulfillment?

"Pleased to Crush Him"?

Stock answers are easy to find. Some say God in His sovereignty just ordained it this way—period. That He gives greater enlightenment to some than to others simply because He has chosen to do so. Matthew 11:21-22 would appear to support this idea. Jesus, with sharp criticism of two cities by the Sea of Galilee where so many miracles had been performed, said these words:

> Woe to you, Chorazin! Woe to you, Bethsaida! For if the miracles had occurred in Tyre and Sidon which occurred in you, they would have repented long ago in sackcloth and ashes.

But Jesus never performed miracles in Tyre and Sidon to the same extent as He did in Galilee. Why *didn't* He—if He knew they would have responded? I do not know.

Others would emphasize the human factor by saying that the Lord will not mock an individual's privilege of saying "no" to God. This too has scriptural support in the fact that it is possible for a person to insult the Spirit of grace (Hebrews 10:29). We are also told that Jesus grieved over the city of Jerusalem because her people—by their own choice—had rejected Him (Matthew 23:37).

With the mention of these seemingly opposing options, we swing the door wide open for theologians to rush in to argue their cases. It's remarkable how creative we humans can be in bringing God's mysteries down low enough to fit into our neat theological systems.

Maybe it's not too late to shut the door long enough to raise a different question that is far more crucial.

I'm quite sure that if you and I could really catch a glimpse of the wrath of God against sin, our question would not be why it is so dark, but why there should be any light from God at all! How could a God of such holy dread still maintain His integrity and show *any* kindness to this evil world? All of us have a long way to go to hate sin and love holiness as much as He does. That distance is perhaps the biggest single reason for our longing that God would show more grace than He has.

Ours is the God who struck Uzzah dead for touching the ark of the Covenant—even though he was trying to help.

Ours is the God who sought to put Moses to death because he had failed to circumcise his son.

Ours is the God who struck Ananias and Sapphira dead in their tracks because they lied about how much they put in the offering.

How do you feel when you read stories like that?

But the ultimate example of God's hatred of sin is found in what He did to His beloved Son. Is it possible for us to even begin to comprehend that huge mass of burning indignation against sin that hung over our Lord Jesus as they nailed Him to the cross? The Bible tells us when Jesus "became sin" that "the LORD was pleased to crush Him, putting Him to grief" (Isaiah 53:10).

"*Pleased* to crush Him"? The Son of His love? I can't handle that. Can you?

Last night, after spending several hours focusing on God's wrath, I went out east of the city for a walk under the stars to try to calm my own inner turmoil. At first I could scarcely lift my head—I was so pressed down by the contrast between His rigid, white-hot moral law and my own far less-than-perfect life. How could I rejoice in my salvation when I knew how often I had failed Him? How could I take pleasure in His love?

Searching for an answer, my mind turned to those verses in Isaiah about God's thoughts and ways being as far above ours as heaven is above the earth. Then I remembered the amazing *context* in which those verses are found.

Seek the LORD while He may be found;
Call upon Him while He is near.
Let the wicked forsake his way,
And the unrighteous man his thoughts;
And let him return to the LORD,
And He will have compassion on him;
And to our God,
For He will abundantly pardon.
For my thoughts are not your thoughts . . .
(Isaiah 55:6-8)

As Isaiah wrote those words he must have wondered, How could a holy God do that? How could He "abundantly pardon" sinful people? His unbending wrath demanded punishment and death. (Remember: Isaiah lived seven hundred years before Calvary.)

And how does God respond? First he tells us that His resources are not restricted by the low level of our intelligence. That's a relief!

What human being ever would have dreamed what God in His highest wisdom had in mind to do? That His plan was to pour out all of His vented wrath upon the Son of His love instead of upon us? That He had chosen a plan in which They—both Father and Son—would suffer the most? Such thoughts are indeed as high above yours and mine as heaven is above the earth!

For He will abundantly pardon.
"For my thoughts *are not* your thoughts,
Neither are your ways My ways," declares the LORD.
"For as the heavens are higher than the earth,
So are My ways higher than your ways,
And My thoughts than your thoughts.
(Isaiah 55:7-9)

"Pardon." "Abundant pardon!" Stopping my walk, and lifting my hands as high toward heaven as I could, I whispered out, "Oh, what a God You are! In Your highest wisdom You found a way to pardon me! Pardon big enough to quench the last trace of Your wrath toward me."

"So shall My word be which goes forth from My mouth;
It shall not return to Me empty,
Without accomplishing what I desire,
And without succeeding in the matter for which I sent it.

For you will go out with joy,
And be led forth with peace;
The mountains and the hills will break forth
    into shouts of joy before you,
And all the trees of the field will clap their hands."
                                        (Isaiah 55:11-12)

"Yes, Lord! I have heard Your word of pardon which has gone forth. I drink it in! Oh thank You! Forever I will thank You."

Gazing up at the myriad stars, it was almost as though I actually *could* hear that voice as it continues to echo on and on around our globe—"I will pardon you . . . pardon you . . . pardon you . . ." Suddenly a breeze surged through a stand of quaking aspens in the meadow where I stood. It was as though they were joining me in my response of joy.

As I listened, peace flooded my heart once more.

The Priceless Commodity

Oh, the grace of my God! "Greater than all my sin!" Yes, His promise of grace has gone forth from His mouth. I have heard it; you have heard it. It continues to go forth. And that word of grace will not return to God without accomplishing *everything* He desires—"without succeeding in the matter for which He sent it." God's purposes of mercy in the midst of wrath will be successful—perfectly successful.

    Shout for joy, O daughter of Zion!
    Shout in triumph, O Israel!
    Rejoice and exult with all your heart,
    O daughter of Jerusalem!
    The LORD has taken away His judgments against you.
                                        (Zephaniah 3:14-15)

You and I may be sure that if it were possible for God to show one more ounce of mercy—to lessen the world's suffering by even one tear—He would do it. We may rest in the fact that God cannot not offer one speck more of His grace than He has and still remain true to His own perfection. His eternal purposes are already running at the level of maximum grace.

What more can anyone say? Yet there is more.

To think that God would allow us—you and me—to stand at the crossroads of the broad and the narrow ways. To be dispensers of such precious, delicately balanced grace purchased at such awful cost. To be privileged to offer to anyone willing to receive. To shine as lights in the midst of the dark fury of both man's sin and God's wrath!

May all of us who handle this priceless commodity—the gracious goodness of God to those who deserve His wrath—do so most carefully.

Chapter 14

All that He Is, He Is to Me

Trust.

So much is wrapped up in that word. It's the very heart of the Christian life—a master key that opens a thousand doors. Think of the times you and I have said, "I wish I could just *trust* the Lord more than I do!" Perhaps like me you have watched someone else stepping out in faith to claim the promises of God, and you felt a strange combination of admiration and guilt. It's an uncomfortable feeling. *Why can't I be that way?*

Sometimes this whole "trusting" thing becomes so complicated. Yes, I want to trust God, but I don't want to become like some who act as though God were their slave, their Aladdin's lamp. What a tragedy if God relinquished His wise purposes and consented to be our robot, instantly obeying all our creative "faith" commands:

> "God, I believe You will heal me from this sickness."
> "God, I really believe You'll give me an 'A' on this exam."
> "God, I know You'll let our home sell by June the third."
> "God, I trust You to let me win the Reader's Digest Sweepstakes . . .
> and I'm even willing to tithe my two-million-dollar prize."

For a few moments, let's set aside the swirl of issues that surround the question of trusting God to do specific things. Instead, let's go deeper. Let's see if we can discover the bedrock on which to build the kind of growing, contagious trust God intends for us.

To do this, we will need to travel to the wilderness of Sinai, east of Egypt and south of Palestine. We will also have to travel in time—3,400 years into the past.

In a rather obscure corner of that great arid region we encounter an old, barefooted shepherd, hiding his face as he stands before a desert bush . . . a bush that blazes with unearthly fire. From the midst of the flame, a voice speaks. Listen.

> I am the God of your father, the God of Abraham, the God of Isaac, and the God of Jacob. . . . I have surely seen the affliction of My people who are in Egypt. . . . So I have come down to deliver them. . . . Therefore, come now, and I will send you to Pharaoh, so that you may bring My people, the sons of Israel, out of Egypt. . . . Certainly I will be with you. (Exodus 3:6-12)

Then the shepherd, Moses, speaks.

> Behold, I am going to the sons of Israel, and I shall say to them, "The God of your fathers has sent me to you." Now they may say to me, "What is His name?" What shall I say to them? (3:13)

God's next words are far more than a simple answer. They are a statement of truth as big as God Himself—truth that puts explosive force into every aspect of His character.

> And God said to Moses, "I AM WHO I AM"; and He said, "Thus you shall say to the sons of Israel, 'I AM has sent me to you' . . . This is My name forever, and this is My memorial-name to all generations." (3:14-15)

I AM.

The words are cloaked in mystery. Sometime after the close of the Old Testament some Jewish rabbis concluded that this name was too sacred to be uttered by sinful human lips. To keep it from being spoken they purposely inserted a different name for God every time the Scriptures were read. Centuries later, when the time came to add vowels to their written Hebrew, the rabbis carefully inserted the wrong ones into God's name. The result was that all future readers would say "Yahowah" rather than as it probably should have been pronounced, "Yahweh." As it was translated into English, "Yahowah" came to be "Jehovah." (In most English versions of the Bible this name appears simply as "LORD.")

While it probably makes little difference to God how we pronounce His name, it must make a great deal of difference to Him that we understand what His name means. There is ample reason to conclude that the name Jehovah is a form of the verb "to be." In all likelihood, God desires us to know that His name means *He will be what He is.*

I remember when I first learned that the words I AM were God's name. *What a letdown*, I thought. Why couldn't God's name be a bit more dramatic . . . like "Supreme Eternal Ruler" . . . or "Merciful Love"? If not those, why not some other familiar Hebrew names for God in those days, such as "Adonai" ("Master") or "Elohim" ("Strong One")?

Apparently the great Pharaoh of Egypt felt just this way when Moses said, "Thus says Jehovah (Yahweh) . . . 'Let My people go.'"

"Who's He? I've never heard of Him. Besides, I will not let Israel go. Maybe, if you had said 'the Crocodile god' or 'Molech' or 'Baal' it might have shaken me up a bit. But 'Yahweh'? That's a new one. Forget it, Moses."

Yet it was not to be forgotten. In the days that followed Pharaoh discovered the hard way that God indeed was *what He is.* As the dreadful plagues descended, Pharaoh learned that Moses' God was a God of *power.* He was a God of *justice* and punishing *wrath.* God was to Pharaoh what HE IS.

To His covenant people crossing the trackless wilderness, God was *faithfulness.* He was *compassion* in the giving of the manna and water from the rock. *Wisdom* and *holiness* in the giving of the Law. *Grace* at the brazen altar. *Patience* in their forty years of wandering. His name is Jehovah. Throughout the rest of the Bible, and throughout all eternity, God WILL BE TO US WHAT HE IS.

What a name! What a most remarkable name. A name that includes in it *everything God is.*

Little wonder that we read,

O LORD, our Lord,
How excellent is Your *name* in all the earth.
$$\text{(Psalm 8:1 NKJV)}$$

and

He leads me in the paths of righteousness
For His *name's* sake.
$$\text{(Psalm 23:3 NKJV)}$$

Little wonder that we hear Jesus saying,

Now My soul is troubled, and what shall I say? "Father, save Me from the hour"? But for this purpose I came to this hour. Father, glorify Your *name*. (John 12:27-28 NKJV)

"This hour" was the cross. Jesus knew that if He were to be the Savior of the world, He must receive to Himself the vileness of the sins of the whole world. This is why He cried out in the garden, "Let this cup pass from Me!" It was not because of His fear of pain, but because He knew that at the moment He "became sin," His Father would become His punishing Judge. "Yes, Father, glorify Your name: *You-will-be-to-me-what-You-are*. You who have always been *love* to Me, will instead become infinite *wrath* and eternal *punishing justice*. Yet it is for this cause I came."

Years later the apostle Paul could write,

For God has not destined us for wrath, but for obtaining salvation through our Lord Jesus Christ. (1 Thessalonians 5:9)

Because of Jesus, our God is now free to be to us *Everything-that-He-is,* without wrath! This is His name forever!

And they shall see His face, and *His name* shall be on their foreheads. And there shall no longer be any night; and they shall not have need of a lamp nor the light of the sun, because the Lord God shall illumine them; and they shall reign forever and ever. (Revelation 22:4-5)

Imagine with me that you are in the hospital awaiting surgery planned for the next morning. The rush of being admitted and the excitement of this strange place have now passed. Visiting hours are over. There you lie—alone. Fears which up to now you were able to hide burst to the surface. Your heart pounds, your skin is flushed. What will be the outcome? What will the pain be like? Will life ever be the same?

Suddenly a neatly dressed gentleman walks into your room carrying a black bag. Stepping closer to your bed and peering into your face he asks,

"You're frightened, aren't you?"

"Oh yes! I really am. This is my first time in the hospital and I'm worried about how the surgery will come out in the morning."

"Listen to me," the man says, "I'm here to tell you that you have nothing to worry about. Everything is going to work out just fine. You will be fit as a fiddle before you know it!"

Just about the moment you begin to relax in those wonderful words—the words you so wanted to hear—the man walks over to the corner of your room, opens up his black bag, and begins repairing the TV set.

Right words, but wrong man!

A while later, another neatly dressed gentleman walks into your room. Coming closer to your bed, he looks down on your troubled face.

"You're frightened, aren't you?"

"Yes, I *really* am. This is my first time in the hospital and I'm worried about how the surgery will come out tomorrow morning."

"Listen to me," the man says, "I'm here to tell you that you have nothing to worry about. Everything is going to work out just fine. You will be fit as a fiddle before you know it!"

"And who are *you?*"

"I'm the doctor who will be doing the surgery on you in the morning. I've checked with great care all the X-rays and blood tests. I've gone over every detail. This is a surgery I have performed dozens of times before with no problems at all. You have nothing to fear. I want you to trust me that everything is going to be all right."

The same words—but oh, what a difference!

No matter how wonderful the promises are—

Peace I leave with you; My peace I give to you; not as the world gives, do I give to you. Let not your heart be troubled, nor let it be fearful. (John 14:27)

—it is the character of the One who speaks them which makes all the difference!

For I am the LORD (Jehovah) your God,
Who upholds your right hand,
Who says to you, "Do not fear, I will help you."
(Isaiah 41:13)

No, it isn't just anyone who says these words. It is "I AM WHO I AM": *The-One-who-will-be-to-me-what-He-is.*

HE says, "Do not fear." And so it will always be.

In my weakness, He will be omnipotence.

In my loneliness, He will be omnipresence.

In my inability to know what I should do, He will be my wisdom.

In my sorrow, He will be my joy.

In my mortality, He will be my life.

At a time of deep personal agony, the pioneer missionary Hudson Taylor received a letter from a friend who wrote the following words—words which radically changed the rest of his life.

> But how to get faith strengthened? Not by striving after faith, but by resting on the Faithful One.

That's it! Trust—faith—is not something we try to pump up full enough to carry the weight of our needs. It is not some sort of mental gymnastics I use to bolster my claim on God's action. It is simply affirming—and resting—in the faithfulness of God to be to me what His promises say He will be. And what is the basis for such restful confidence?

His NAME.

The very name of God.

Chapter 15

"God . . . Wow!"

Worship.

What images does that word bring to mind? Shafts of light through stained glass windows? Reverberating pipe organs? Choirs, robes, candles, and incense?

What *is* worship? Just another word for praise or thanksgiving? Something fulfilled by attending a "worship service" once a week?

To find out, let's look at two familiar yet radically different worship stories in the Bible.

Two Who Worshiped

In 2 Chronicles 20 the nation of Judah was threatened with total destruction by the simultaneous invasion of three large enemy armies. There was no conceivable way King Jehoshaphat could save his people. There was no hope and he knew it . . . unless God intervened.

As all Judah gathered, "standing before the LORD, with their infants, their wives, and their children," the good king confessed, "We are powerless before this great multitude who are come against us; nor do we know what to do, but our eyes are on Thee (20:12-13).

In that electric moment of despair, a prophet stood up with a word from God: "Do not fear or be dismayed . . . for the battle is not yours, but God's. . . . You need not fight in this battle; station yourselves, stand and see the salvation of the LORD on your behalf" (20:15-17).

The next thing we see is Jehoshaphat and all of Judah falling down with their faces to the ground "worshiping the LORD."

With that moment in history still fresh in our minds, let's turn to a story that could scarcely be more opposite.

The story of Job begins with a scene full of life and peace and joyful expectation. Then with shattering suddenness his entire world falls apart (Job 1:13-19). In a few minutes' time four catastrophes roar into Job's life, wiping out all his material possessions—and killing all his children.

Then we read, "Job arose and tore his robe and shaved his head, and he fell to the ground and worshiped."

Jehoshaphat and Job both fell with their faces to the ground and worshiped. But how could the circumstances have been more different? Worship, then, is just as fitting when you hear the voice of God fulfilling your dreams . . . as it is when you feel His hand destroying them. It belongs in the midst of overwhelming joy as well as in overwhelming grief.

A God Too Big

What then is worship? To simply say that it is thanking God or praising Him in every circumstance may be missing its essence. Let's take a second, closer look at these two stories.

What did Jehoshaphat really expect from God when he prayed? A word from the LORD? A promise of victory? Yes, God had done that before. Perhaps God would promise extra boldness to his soldiers. Perhaps, as with Gideon's army, He would reveal some special military tactic. But no, *this time God would do it all*. All! This was more, so much more than Jehoshaphat had dared to dream! His was a God *too big*. This was something bigger and more marvelous than his small brain could handle.

What then do you do when you are confronted with a God too big? Two things: You get as low as you can—as small as you can before a God too awesome to grasp; and in that smallness you respond—because you can't do anything else *but* respond.

For me, one word best sums up that response. Worship is saying "Wow!" to God. Worship isn't a song we sing. In fact, you may not say anything at all—for how do you say a "gasp"? Maybe "Wow" doesn't sound like a very sacred word to you. If so, change it. But don't miss the point: Worship is not so much words as it is *your automatic response out of your own utter smallness to a God too big.*

Too big to wrap your mind around.

Too big to figure out.

If you suddenly found yourself before a giant, would you try to stand tall, stretching up as high as you could in order to feel more his equal? Or would you find yourself sort of hunching your shoulders, pressed down by the immensity before you? Before a God too big the only place to be is low, as low as you can get. This is exactly what the primary Hebrew word for worship originally meant—"bowing low."

King Jehoshaphat bowed low. But how was it with Job? It was just the same. No, there was no joy, no sudden excitement, no tingle of exhilaration. There was just one lone man with a crushed heart within his own shattered world. Yet he too found himself confronted with a God *too big*—too sovereign, too mysterious, too much beyond anything Job could figure out. What had happened could not have been coincidence—sheer chance. No, in some incomprehensible way, his God was involved. And Job tore his clothes, fell to the ground and said "Wow!"

Worship is always that way. Whether around the throne of God in heaven where we read of the living creatures and the elders who "fell down and worshiped" (Revelation 4:10, 5:14, and 19:4), or whether it is one man by a well in Mesopotamia who "bowed low and worshiped" (Genesis 24:26). Always, eternally, in every circumstance, whenever a believer allows himself to be confronted by His God—really confronted—he will worship. Because God, rightly perceived, will always be a God *too big*. Too big in His forgiveness. Too big in His love. Too big in His judgments. Too big in His grace. Whatever we discover Him to be, He is far too big for us in our utter smallness to grasp. We can't handle it. We weren't made to handle it. We were made to worship.

I wonder—as the hosts of heaven look down on this most special

planet and observe the children of God—if they are not appalled
by the absence of worship. We, of all His creatures, should be most
in awe. We alone have tasted God's grace and forgiveness. We alone
have been taken out of the kingdom of darkness into the kingdom
of light. We alone are the bride of the Son of God.

Taking Time to Be Overwhelmed

If worship is not happening among God's people today it may
be because we have shaped our concepts of God to fit the limits of
our understanding—measuring God by our own intellect. We feel
quite free to expect answers from Him to all our "whys"—as though
we assume our brains are adequate to handle His answers. We "worship" only when we decide God has lived up to our expectations.
And having brought Him down to our level, there is little reason
for falling with our faces to the ground. He is no longer a God too
big.

Do we Christians actually do this? Think back to the last time
you were a bit disappointed with God because something you so
hoped for and dreamed of was not taking place. You had even gone
to the effort of doing all the "ground work," preparing the way for
God to act. You figured, planned, and even prayed—hard. In fact,
the part you were asking God to do was really not much at all,
especially for Him.

But why didn't God cooperate? Didn't He know of your "solution"? Imagine you're a little child trying to climb over a wall.
Working so hard, you make against the base of the wall a pile of
stones to stand on, and you can almost reach the top—but not quite.
Really all you need is just a little boost from Daddy. Just a boost!
You're already most of the way there; you've already done most of
the work. But for some reason Daddy isn't doing it. Doesn't he love
you? Doesn't he care?

If only in such moments we could stop our anxiety long enough
to hear again the voice of God . . .

For as the heavens are higher than the earth,
So are My ways higher than your ways,
And My thoughts than your thoughts.

Isn't it amazing? Our disappointments in not seeing God "come up" to our expectations are because we have not been looking high enough to see a God *above* our expectations.

Closely related to this is the fact that many of us who have studied the Bible for years succumb to the subtle danger of dividing biblical truth between the FATHOMABLE, or understandable, and the UNFATHOMABLE, that which we cannot understand.

The "fathomables" would include the basic facts of the gospel and the basic mechanics of the Christian life. At the same time we would agree that mysteries like the Trinity, the sovereignty of God and the free will of man, or the divine and human natures of Christ fall into the "unfathomable" category. After all, better minds than ours have been wrestling with those issues for hundreds of years and haven't solved much. But as for the rest of the Bible . . . if you study real hard, you can get a handle on it.

You can put the gospel into four simple statements: GOD'S PO-SITION, MAN'S CONDITION, GOD'S PROVISION, MAN'S DECISION. Justification is easy; think of it as: Just-if-I'd-never-sinned. And you can sew up the grace of God into a neat acronym: G-R-A-C-E . . . *GOD'S RICHES AT CHRIST'S EXPENSE.*

"No!" shouts Paul (see Romans 11:33). The grace of God is un-fathomable. The riches of Christ are unsearchable. The ways of God are unreachable. Worship as you read. Tremble as you teach!

Yes, God has cracked open the door to His room of mystery, and given us a peek. Yet even if the door were wide open, and we gazed for a million billion years, we would still tremble before the sight.

But allowing yourself to be overwhelmed with God takes time. And where's a person to find time these days anyway? Not only that, but my emotions are drained from watching "M.A.S.H." reruns on TV.

What if you start taking your life with God as seriously as He takes it? Seriously enough to save the best of your thinking and the best of your emotions for Him? Following this paragraph is a series of phrases from Scripture—mind-stretching, heart-touching phrases. What would happen if you took time today— now—to mull over each one . . . checking through the chapters in which each is found . . . allowing God enough time to paint the artistry of His truth on

your heart . . . seeing each one as a masterpiece of His greatness . . .
giving your imagination free reign to see them as deeper, higher, and
wider truths than you have ever seen before?

Thanks be to God for His indescribable gift . . .
(2 Corinthians 9:15)

The surpassing greatness of His power . . .
(Ephesians 1:19)

The surpassing riches of His grace . . .
(Ephesians 2:7)

The unfathomable riches of Christ . . .
(Ephesians 3:8)

The love of Christ which surpasses knowledge . . .
(Ephesians 3:19)

With joy inexpressible and full of glory . . .
(1 Peter 1:8)

An eternal weight of glory far beyond all comparison . . .
(2 Corinthians 4:17)

No, you didn't plan to kneel, to press your face into the rug. And
the tears? They weren't planned either. But that's where you find
yourself—low before the Most High.

Emotional Substitutes for Worship

Another subtle reason why real worship isn't more common
among God's people is that we have quite innocently created emotional substitutes for it. You see, we human beings are capable of
making other things which are "too big." Sometimes we do that
with music. From gifted composers and performers has come music
so moving as to emotionally sweep us off our feet. Perhaps we
intended God to be our focus, but all too often, it was nothing
more than the experience that was "too big."

Remember the last time you sat in an acoustically perfect au-
ditorium waiting to hear some great choir? The curtain opens, the
audience hushes and then . . . SOUND! It really would not have
made any difference if the choir's first word had been "Halibut"
instead of "Hallelujah." For at that moment, experience—not
truth—was center stage, an experience a non-Christian could have
enjoyed equally as well as you.

It takes a truly worship-focused, truth-focused, Spirit-led musician
to point people through the music to experience the real thing.

No, Gothic towers, stained glass windows and glorious choirs are not wrong at all—God originated beauty—but they dare not become poor substitutes for your privilege of being "swept away" by discovering the glory and greatness of your God.

Perhaps next Sunday in church you will be allowed a few moments of uninterrupted time to mull over the mystery of this "Great God of Wonders." Sitting next to you may be a Jehoshaphat who feels like shouting "Glory!" to a God too kind, too tender, too loving. Yet you may be a Job, crushed with grief. Whatever fragile crutches you had have been stripped away. No more figuring, planning, dreaming—only the wasting exhaustion of the nothingness that remains. Inwardly falling to your face you whisper "wow." Not in anger or rebellion, but rather in awe before a most mysterious God who in the darkness that doesn't seem to be making any sense, still says "I love you."

Experiencing the "O" Grade

When I was a boy our family often went camping in the High Sierras in California. Traveling along the eastern slopes of those ten- to fourteen-thousand-foot peaks involved several steep grades and dry, desertlike heat. Steaming radiators and canvas water bags slung over car bumpers were standard equipment.

One mountain grade I will never forget. It had a funny name: the "O" grade.

"Why?" I asked my father, "Why is it called that way? Is the next grade after it the 'P' grade?" Mom and Dad simply smiled and said, "Just wait. You'll see."

Up and UP we would climb on the twisting switchback road through scrub pine and sage. And then—when it seemed we would never get to the top of the ridge—we did! Spontaneously I cried out "Oh!" There in front of us, beyond a diamond-studded lake and framed with quaking aspen, was the jagged, snowy Sierra Crest . . . higher, more massive, more beautiful, more alive with color than I had dreamed.

We all laughed together at our now-shared secret. Someday, I thought to myself, I would have the chance to say to someone else, "Just wait. You'll see!"

Instead of the Sierra Crest, picture in your mind a great symphonic production in a concert hall. Can you see it? Hear it? Now, remove all the audience. Then, make all the musicians stone deaf. What remains?

Is the symphony still being played? Are sound waves still carrying music throughout the great hall? Yes. But with no one hearing, it is as though nothing is happening at all.

Our God has ordained that His children down here on our tiny planet are to be both the listening participants and the responding audience to the symphony of His majesty—the vast panorama of His greatness. Jesus once said, "I tell you, if these become silent, the stones will cry out!"

God has a limitless store of "O" grades for each of us. Often they will come suddenly, unexpectedly, when we find ourselves confronted with the stark immensity of our most mysterious God—His grace, His forgiveness, His patience, His creativity, His friendship, His judgment. Sometimes they will come at the end of what we feared was an endless "grade" of suffering.

But most of God's "O" grades are ours right now—this moment—when we simply choose to pause and contemplate any of the myriad facets of the character of our God. And bowing low, trembling, we will once more discover a God *too big*.